POWERFUL PEACE

How the peace of Christ can help you achieve
God's best for your life and your relationships!

by Greg & Sharon Fletcher

For ordering information,
please contact bookorders@pwmin.org
or order online at www.gods-best.com.

Dedication and Appreciation

We would like to dedicate this book to our children, Joshua, Hannah, Isaac, and Judah, for being great motivating factors in our desire for wanting peace in our home. You have a prophet's reward for your efforts and hard work. We are awed by your willingness to serve the Lord.

Above everything, all praise and honor goes to our loving Father, amazing Lord Jesus Christ, and the wonderful Holy Spirit for teaching us and helping us to write this message.

Table of Contents

Greg and I had a pretty normal marriage the first few years. We collected a few dogs, a few kids, a few cars, a house, and were well on our way to our slice of the American Dream. Unfortunately, during our first 8 years of marriage, we had never really learned to live in peace with each other and become the unified unit God purposed when He put us together. We were just two roommates living in the same house and sharing parenting and cleaning responsibilities. We were falling further and further out of "love" with each other as we saw more and more things about each other that we didn't like. We weren't forgiving each other and we were making life harder for one another by our poor choices.

It was no surprise to either of us when it came to a head one day. After hundreds of arguments, I had convinced myself that my children would be happier if we were no longer married. I had packed up the minivan and taken out money from the bank and the kids and I were headed out.

My carefully conceived plan might have worked if I could have reached the garage door opener when Greg unplugged it! Fortunately for all of us, I couldn't, and I had to go back into the house and talk it out with him.

A few months before, we had been given a used copy of Joyce Meyer's book "Life Without Strife" and I had read the first few chapters. I instantly recognized all of the errors my husband had been making in our marriage and made a mental note of them. As we started to try talking instead of my leaving, I saw this book on a night stand and threw it at Greg and told him he needed to read it. He picked it up and went to pray. He came back to me and said we should both read this book for ourselves and just let God speak to us individually about the issues we could clearly see in each other. I agreed. As we both humbled ourselves before God, He began to peel away our foolish pride and show us what we had really been doing to each other and to other people. This book is a culmination of the study on peace, God's love, and the snares the devil uses against believers to steal what is rightfully ours in Christ. We hope it brings you as much freedom as it has given to us and we hope you walk in the fullness of His love and peace for you! —Sharon

Important: Please Read

Introduction and Instructions

How to approach this book and ensure your success:

Through years of teaching this material, we have discovered a few principles that will greatly enhance your ability to utilize it.

1. **Read this material for yourself**. Don't fall for the trap of applying this material to the lives of others! You can only change yourself! You can love and influence others, but only after you are walking in peace in your own life. Remember the flight attendants that tell parents to secure their own oxygen masks before they help their children or those that have needs around them. You have to be in a good place yourself to be able to help others.

2. **You get out of this material what you put into it.** If you only halfheartedly dabble in study and applying God's Word, you will get poor results. God deserves your whole heart and if you really apply these truths, God will lead you to a radical freedom and peace and alter the landscape of your life.

3. **Be Courageous**. Don't be afraid to allow the Holy Spirit to lead you into greater freedoms in your life, even when the path seems painful and the payoff seems miles away. It isn't! Be confident and let him lead you into His peace and freedom knowing that He loves you, and is leading you into a greater and more fruitful life.

4. **Do not rush through the reading of this book**. We know there are many people that are able to read through a book at a single sitting, but please don't! Real change and receiving from God takes time. Rushing through may seem pleasurable, but you might sacrifice your opportunity to grow. We want you to be able to apply this material as the Holy Spirit reveals things to you. As you start reading, listen for the Holy Spirit to bear witness with your spirit concerning a concept you are studying. Stay there for awhile and study it, reread the section or chapter. Meditate on the scriptures in that section. If a particular section of a chapter doesn't speak to you, that's ok too. But please don't read more than one chapter every other day. You simply will not absorb this material that way. You need to absorb this material in order for you to see the fruit. Reread often, especially if you have been distracted or too busy to really give it your full attention. We recommend leaving this book out and

visible as a reminder and encouragement of all you have learned.

If you are the type of person who likes to read a whole book first to get the gist of it, please re-read it slowly afterwards to allow the Holy Spirit to really work the material into your life. We have seen this be very fruitful.

5. **Be patient**. This material may require a lot of you. Be patient with yourself and allow the Holy Spirit free reign to lead you and teach you. It is worth it!

6. **Be prepared to meet some resistance**. There are truths in this book that can set you free. Don't expect the enemy to give up a foothold in your life without a fight. He has kept you ignorant of his schemes and he wants to keep it that way. The good news is that he has no power over you to keep you from all that God has for you. Let the Holy Spirit lead you into peace and glorious freedom to resist the enemy!

WHAT IS PEACE?

What does the world say peace is?

To some people, the word "peace" might conjure scenes of a sloping meadow bathed in sunshine with birds chirping and a quiet brook gently gurgling in the background. To children of the sixties, peace might mean tolerance of others, no rules, and no war. To the military, peace might mean a permanent cease-fire between two warring countries or groups. To parents, peace might mean content and sleeping children at the end of a busy day. We use the terms "peace and quiet" to represent an absence of conflict or busyness. Is this what the word *peace* really means?

Does peace depend on our circumstances?

Sometimes we think, "If this one thing will happen, I can have peace..." or, "Once I have money in the bank I can have peace..." or, "Once my family is all saved..." or, "Once I get the promotion at work I want..." or, "Once my kids move out..." or, "Once I get a new car or a bigger house...."

What are some things you are waiting for to enjoy peace?

When Jesus spoke to His disciples in the book of John He said, "Peace I leave with you, My peace I give to you; not as the world gives do I give to you." (John 14:27 NKJV) These are part of the last recorded words He spoke to His disciples before His death on the cross, so we know they are important. The disciples had seen Jesus remain peaceful and even sleep in the midst of frightening storms and hardships.

They had seen Him remain restful and composed as crowds drew from Him on a daily basis. They witnessed His calm demeanor as He faced down angry Pharisees and religious leaders that felt threatened and purposefully tried to verbally trip Him up with their questioning. He was about to face the hardest challenge of His life and do so with amazing peace and strength. He goes on to say, "These things I have spoken to you, that in Me you may have peace. In the world you will have tribulation; but be of good cheer, I have overcome the world." (John 16:33 NKJV) It sounds like the peace He bequeathed to us is a very powerful thing. It also sounds like it doesn't have anything to do with our current circumstances. In the Word, we are instructed to "guard our peace"(Eph. 4:3), "let the peace of Christ rule in our hearts"(Col. 3:15), and "be led forth by peace"(Isaiah 55:12). Jesus's idea of peace and the world's are very, very different. God's kind of peace isn't dependent on our circumstances, but supersedes them and changes them according to His will for us.

When I turned 18, I decided to completely turn my life over to Christ and just see what He could do if I totally submitted to His will in all areas of my life. I was certain that if somehow, I could completely obey God in all things, that He would cause me to be blessed in every area of my life and be victorious. I then spent the next 15 or so years trying to get my flesh and my family and friends to follow what I thought was God's will in order to try and somehow get God's best for all of us. I stressed myself out every time my circumstances didn't line up with what I thought was God's will, which was almost all of the time! I made life rough for everyone around me while trying to fulfill God's plan for us. I sincerely believed, and still do, that God's will is the absolute best plan for everyone. However, I was trying to "strong-arm" my circumstances to be in line with what I thought God wanted, and sacrificing my peace in the process. It took me 15 or more years to finally give up trying to control my circumstances and just trust in my loving Heavenly Father to fulfill His perfect will in my life. I tend to be pretty stubborn, so I think it took me that long to figure out it didn't work! —Sharon

The Need for Peace

Before we can outline God's definition of peace, we must first contrast this with where we were before salvation came into the world. It is important to note that when Adam and Eve disobeyed God's instructions in the Garden of Eden, a huge chasm was formed between God and His children. His original purpose for mankind was to enjoy close fellowship with Him, and this separation grieved Him. He saw the ravages of sin and its consequences of separation, death, disease, lack, and strife.

> *He saw that there was no man, And wondered that there was no intercessor; Therefore His own arm brought salvation for Him; And His own righteousness, it sustained Him.*
> *Isaiah 59:16 (NKJV)*

But thankfully God, like it says in John 3:16, loved us so much that He sent His only Son to bridge the gap. Through Jesus' obedience and death on the cross, the peace of God was established back on the Earth.

> *For it pleased the Father that in Him all the fullness should dwell, and by Him to reconcile all things to Himself, by Him, whether things on earth or things in heaven, having made peace through the blood of His cross. Col. 1:19-20 (NKJV)*

This scripture shows us how Jesus purchased reconciliation between us and God the Father, and restored of all the benefits of that relationship that were lost in the Garden of Eden. This is the peace that Jesus came, lived, and died to give us.

When Jesus gave us that amazing promise of peace we find in John 14, He was probably speaking in Hebrew to His Jewish disciples. We can therefore learn even more about what peace means by looking at the Hebrew word for peace —*shalom*. Shalom means many things in Hebrew including:

- Wholeness
- Health
- Peace
- Welfare
- Safety
- Soundness
- Tranquility

- Prosperity
- Perfectness
- Fullness
- Rest
- Harmony
- The absence of agitation or discord

As you can see here, Shalom (peace) is not some weak, passive concept but a rich fabric of life's most important aspects. We would love to have every one of these things overflowing in our lives!

Peace is not simply a lack of conflict but it is a powerful, active force moving us forward into everything God has planned for us. In our pre-Jesus state, we spend our whole lives in a perpetual state of poverty and death. We have no real love, no true joy, and are conditioned to believe that lack and guilt are normal. In a proper relationship with God through Jesus Christ, God's normal for us is full of joy, love, peace, blessing, and freedom (Romans 14:17).

Some of these benefits include:

- Unbroken fellowship with the Father
- Comfort and presence of the Holy Spirit
- Wisdom for life's issues
- Blessings both spiritual and physical
- Purpose in life
- Protection from the enemy and trouble
- All the benefits Jesus walked in while on the Earth

Like most young married couples, Sharon and I were in love with each other but struggled to have peace in our relationship. After a while, I started to notice patterns of behavior. During the week, when we were both at work, we would get along great, but on the weekend we would fight and struggle. I started asking myself and Sharon why this was so. At first, the answers always seemed to be that it was the other person who was making life unbearable, but it never really sat right in my heart. I loved Jesus, she loved Jesus, we were both born-again but for some reason, we were lacking the victory the Word told us we should have. It was about this time that we started learning about strife and peace. God began really challenging Sharon and me to trust in Him for victory and stop sabotaging our marriage and life together by giving into the enemy's ploys. This transformed our relationship and set us on a path that has blessed us so much. Today, we walk in peace in our home and marriage and I am more in love with her than when we were first married. God is amazing and His Word always works!
—Greg

Why We Need Peace

We need the presence of God in our lives. We were created by God to love Him and enjoy Him forever. Walking in the peace of God is walking continually conscious of His presence and guidance. Jesus is our peace and has paved the way for us to have **unlimited access to God**.

> *Therefore let us draw near with confidence to the throne of grace,*
> *so that we may receive mercy and find grace to help in time of need.*
> *Hebrews 4:16 (NASB)*

We need **protection from the attacks of the enemy**. Philippians 4:6-7 says,

> *Be anxious for nothing, but in everything by prayer and supplication,*
> *with thanksgiving, let your requests be made known to God;*
> *and the peace of God, which surpasses all understanding, will guard*
> *your hearts and minds through Christ Jesus. (NASB)*

We see here that the peace of God actually guards our hearts and minds when we abide and trust in Him. We need **God's help in the affairs of life,** to make good and wise decisions. Paul encourages us in the book of Colossians to lean on Jesus and His peace when he says,

> *And let the peace (soul harmony which comes) from Christ rule (act*
> *as umpire continually) in your hearts [deciding and settling with*
> *finality all questions that arise in your minds, in that peaceful state]*
> *to which as [members of Christ's] one body you were also called [to*
> *live]. And be thankful. Colossians 3:15 (AMP)*

God's peace helps us hear Him and make decisions based on His value system. When we let the peace of God reign in our hearts, He will show us where to go, what to say, what to do, and how to be. He will keep us out of trouble! He will keep us safe! He will lead us into His blessings!

Peace allows God to work for us on our behalf. Psalm 91 is a wonderful psalm depicting the blessings that come to the one who makes the Lord his refuge and trust. His promises to us are:

> *You shall not be afraid of the terror of the night, nor of the arrow*
> *(the evil plots and slanders of the wicked) that flies by day, nor of the*
> *pestilence that stalks in darkness, nor of the destruction and sudden*

death that surprise and lay waste at noonday. A thousand may fall at your side, and ten thousand at your right hand, but it shall not come near you. Only a spectator shall you be [yourself inaccessible in the secret place of the Most High] as you witness the reward of the wicked. Because you have made the Lord your refuge, and the Most High your dwelling place, there shall no evil befall you, nor any plague or calamity come near your tent. Because he has set his love upon Me, therefore I will deliver him; I will set him on high, because he has known My name. He shall call upon Me, and I will answer him; I will be with him in trouble; I will deliver him and honor him. With long life I will satisfy him, And show him My salvation. Psalm 91:5-10,14-16 (AMP)

When Jesus becomes our peace with God, all these blessings are poured out on us!

How We Get Peace

The good news is that when we accept Jesus as our Lord and Savior, we are automatically brought into His peace! It is a valuable part of the new birth experience, but most people don't know very much about it. In John 14:27, Jesus tells us He left us His peace and it belongs to us now. Isaiah 53:5 states:

But He was wounded for our transgressions, He was bruised for our iniquities; The chastisement for our peace was upon Him, And by His stripes we are healed. Isaiah 53:5 (NKJV)

The payment needed for us to obtain peace was laid upon Jesus. He paid for our peace, in full, on the cross!

Now, as with almost every promise from God, there are two parts: God's part and our part. When Jesus says, in John 14:27, "Peace I leave with you; My peace I give to you; not as the world gives do I give to you. Do not let your heart be troubled, nor let it be fearful" (NASB), you can clearly see these two parts. God's part is to present the peace of Christ, free of charge, as a gift to us as we believe in Jesus. Our part is right after that—to not let our hearts be troubled or fearful (afraid). We can choose to cooperate with Him and receive and walk in the blessings of Christ's peace, or we can let our hearts be troubled and fearful and walk away from those blessings. Either way, the choice is ours to make and the results we see in our lives depend on which option we choose. God's part has already been settled forever in heaven and that gift of peace is always available, but we have to do our part to see it in our own lives daily.

How We Guard Peace

Ephesians 4:3 states,

> *"Make every effort to keep yourselves united in the Spirit, binding yourselves together with peace." (NLT)*

We can see here that there must be something WE can do that affects the peace of God in our lives. 1 Peter 3:10-11 says,

> *For whoever would love life and see good days must keep his tongue from evil and his lips from deceitful speech. He must turn from evil and do good; he must seek peace and pursue it. (NIV)*

Peace can and should be sought after and constantly pursued. We are going to give you the tools to recognize where you may have been giving up the peace that Jesus left you, and we are going to show you how to keep it and rest in it.

Consider where you are sensing God's peace in your life and where it is missing. Make note of those areas.

_____

_____

_____

_____

_____

_____

_____

_____

_____

_____

GOD'S BEST

God's Best for Your Life

Having God's Best in our lives means we are walking and living out Jesus's prayer when He prayed, "Your kingdom come, Your will be done on earth as it is in heaven." God's will for us is always good. His plans for us are always to bless us far beyond all we can ask or think.

It may be foreign to you to consider that God actually wants good things for us and to bless us in every area of our lives, so we are going to practice that mindset right now.

Close your eyes and quiet your mind. Let go of the issues of your day. Now, imagine what God's best for your life would look like. Consider this scripture as you do this. Psalm 84:11 states,

> *For the Lord God is a sun and shield; The Lord gives grace and glory; No good thing does He withhold from those who walk uprightly. (NKJV)*

When Greg and I were new parents, just learning how to walk in faith and believe God for His best in our lives, we were puzzled. We just weren't seeing what we were taught we could expect. We found ourselves giving offerings, tithing, confessing God's Word over our lives, and nothing was getting better. One evening, after a dinner of rice and little else, I demanded Greg go out to talk to God and find out why we weren't seeing the breakthroughs we were believing God for. Greg patiently agreed and went to talk to Jesus and get some wisdom. What he came back with was God's perspective of our strife-filled marriage. - Sharon

We had little to no money. What money we had went toward rent and feeding the children. We tithed and gave offerings and were really approaching God and His word in faith, but the blessings just weren't coming back to us. At some point, Sharon had a moment where she just told me to go find out from God what to do. I really had no idea how to even approach this, but I knew I couldn't stay in the apartment with her, so I went outside and sat down in the stairwell and cried out to God. God showed me an image in my mind of a classic shaker end table. This table had a small top, and was tall with skinny legs. God told me that the table represented our marriage. As I looked closely, I could see that one of the legs was broken and leaned in a bit, which caused the table to lean and be unstable. God told me that He couldn't bless us because our marriage was unstable and couldn't support the weight of what He wanted for us. We had to get our marriage in better shape for God to be able give us His best, because He wasn't going to jeopardize His blessings and our marriage until we did. —Greg

1. Write down some of the "good things" that come to mind. Don't limit them with earthly reasoning or whether you think they are doable. Remember, nothing is impossible with God (Luke 1:37), so don't limit it in any way. James 1:17 states,

> *Every good and perfect gift is from above, coming down from the Father of the heavenly lights, who does not change like shifting shadows. (NIV)*

_____

_____

_____

Let's continue this exercise and try to really focus on specific situations.

2. What would His best look like in your relationships?

> *When a man's ways please the LORD, He makes even his enemies to be at peace with him. Proverbs 16:7 (NKJV)*

_____

_____

_____

_____

3. What about your finances?

Beloved, I pray that you may prosper in all things and be in health, just as your soul prospers. 3 John 1:2 (NKJV)

> *And my God shall supply all your need according to His riches in glory by Christ Jesus. Philippians 4:19 (NKJV)*

_____

_____

_____

_____

4. Your health?

> *And He Himself bore our sins in His body on the cross, so that we might die to sin and live to righteousness; for by His wounds you were healed. 1 Peter 2:24 (NASB)*

---

5. Your marriage?

Your wife shall be like a fruitful vine in the very heart of your house, Your children like olive plants all around your table. Psalm 128:3 (NKJV)

> *Husbands, love your wives, just as Christ also loved the church and gave Himself for her, Ephesians 5:25 (NKJV)*

---

6. Your family?

> *All your children shall be taught by the Lord, And great shall be the peace of your children. Isaiah 54:13 (NKJV)*

---

7. Your work/employment?

> *Do you see a man skilled in his work? He will stand before kings;*
> *He will not stand before obscure men. Proverbs 22:29 (NASB)*

_____

_____

_____

_____

8. Your spiritual maturity?

> *For this reason I bow my knees before the Father, from whom every*
> *family in heaven and on earth derives its name, that He would grant*
> *you, according to the riches of His glory, to be strengthened with power*
> *through His Spirit in the inner man, so that Christ may dwell in your*
> *hearts through faith; and that you, being rooted and grounded in love,*
> *may be able to comprehend with all the saints what is the breadth and*
> *length and height and depth, and to know the love of Christ which*
> *surpasses knowledge, that you may be filled up to all the fullness of*
> *God. Ephesians 3:14-19 (NASB)*

_____

_____

_____

_____

If you've done this right, your list will have some amazing things on it—things you cannot achieve on your own, things that you have wanted your whole life and have maybe struggled to think are even possible. Now contemplate that God's best is far better than what's on your list or anything else you have thought about!

> *Now to Him who is able to do exceedingly abundantly above all that*
> *we ask or think, according to the power that works in us, to Him be*
> *glory in the church by Christ Jesus to all generations, forever and ever.*
> *Amen. Ephesians 3:20-21 (NKJV)*

God truly is a good God! His goodness in our lives is only limited by us. As we continue in this study to learn to walk in Powerful Peace, we will be asked to give up some bad habits and destructive thought patterns. Remembering all that God has for us will encourage us and keep us focused on the prize when we count the cost of following Christ in every area of our lives.

Now that you have a little bit of an idea of what God wants for you and your family, remember those things when the enemy comes and you are tempted to give up your peace. Remember...

> *For we do not wrestle against flesh and blood, but against principalities, against powers, against the rulers of the darkness of this age, against spiritual hosts of wickedness in the heavenly places. Ephesians 6:12 (NKJV)*

God's desire for us is to live so secure in His love for us and His care of us, that we maintain and enjoy His peace in every situation we encounter on this earth. Because of this peace, we are able to trust His good plans and purposes for us in everything. Abiding in the peace of God is a vital part of obtaining His best for our lives. It is a powerful force that protects us and ushers us into the presence of God Almighty in our time of need.

Meditate on these scriptures.

> *Delight yourself also in the Lord, And He shall give you the desires of your heart. Psalm 37:4 (NKJV)*

> *The thief does not come except to steal, and to kill, and to destroy. I have come that they may have life, and that they may have it more abundantly. John 10:10 (NKJV)*

9. In the section below, complete your list of what God's best for you and your family would look like.

_____

_____

_____

_____

THE THIEF OF PEACE

The thief does not come except to steal, and to kill, and to destroy.
I have come that they may have life, and that they may have it more
abundantly. John 10:10 (NKJV)

As we see here in the book of John, the thief, that is Satan, wants to come into our lives and steal the peace and blessings of God. He wants to destroy what God is doing in our lives. Ultimately, the devil wants to kill us, and it all starts with stealing our peace.

Keeping the Peace

Exodus 14:14 states,

> *The Lord will fight for you, and you shall hold your peace and remain*
> *at rest. Exodus 14:14 (AMP)*

Ephesians 4:3 states we should be

> *...endeavoring to keep the unity of the Spirit in the bond of peace.*
> *(AMP)*

If we are to "hold our peace" and "keep the unity of the Spirit in the bond of peace," it stands to reason that we can also put it down and lose it if we aren't careful. We know that the thief comes to steal, kill, and destroy, but often we don't recognize the thief's coming because he uses deception to hide his movements from us. The enemy studies us and crafts the perfect "bait" to get us to let go of our peace and trade it in for what he wants to bring us: death and destruction! As we learn to recognize these patterns in our lives, we will be able to adequately "hold" the peace Jesus suffered and died to leave us, and "keep the unity of the Spirit," by purposely resisting these temptations.

Psalm 91:1 states, "He who dwells in the shelter of the Most High will abide in the shadow of the Almighty" and the rest of the chapter lists out the blessings and comforts that come to the person resting under His care. We like the illustration of standing under an umbrella to show us what that looks like. As it rains sickness, poverty, lack, strife, discontent, and discord outside, it also rains blessings, peace, joy, love, grace, health, protection, and all the amazing gifts we receive in Christ under the umbrella. As we stay nestled up under our Father's care, there is nothing that can harm us and we have a continual feast in His Presence. It is always our choice whether we stay there or not. It is His perfect will that we abide with Him always, but God will not force us to do so. We can leave His loving protection anytime we choose to. We can trade our Christ-bought, God-given peace to play with the toys the devil brings to us instead—and reap the consequences as well!

> Before Greg and I effectively learned how to walk in peace on a consistent basis, we wasted every weekend and many evenings in strife and discord. Everything we had planned for the family seemed impossible to complete and was ten times harder than it should have been. Even cleaning up the kitchen after the evening meal seemed like climbing Mount Everest! Conversations all ended up in arguments and nothing made sense! We would decide to make some home improvements and would end up in a heated discussion, the kids would be fighting in their rooms, and Greg or I would leave the house in a huff and nothing would be fun for anyone! —Sharon

Recognizing Lack of Peace

One of the most important things to learn, when we are attempting to stay in the peace of God on a consistent basis, is to recognize when we have given up God's peace in some area. Strife occurs when we give up the peace of God and give in to the enemy's influence or the influence of our flesh. Strife is defined as "angry or violent struggle; conflict; rivalry or contention, especially of a bitter kind."[1]

Being in strife causes you to spin your wheels and lose effectiveness in the rest of your life, much like a car loses traction on slick surfaces and can't benefit from the power of its engine. Once you get out of strife and back in God's peace, all the horse power that lies within you and which God provides to you can get traction and you can really start to see great things happening in your life! —Greg

Here are some signs we have found that may indicate the presence and influence of strife in our lives:

- Willingness to throw away relationships
- More fatigue/struggle than usual, just to do simple tasks
- Confusion and chaos
- An angry undercurrent in the home
- Children bickering and rebelling
- Lack of God's blessing, i.e. - trouble, after trouble
- Lack of joy and fulfillment or contentment

Unknowingly, we allow the devil to come in and steal our peace, and then wonder why we are so angry, or why things aren't working out the way we see the Bible has promised us. We need to follow Paul's admonition to do whatever it takes,

> So that no advantage would be taken of us by Satan, for we are not ignorant of his schemes. 2 Corinthians 2:11 (NKJV)

From the beginning, the enemy has been a liar, a murderer, and a thief, and his methods haven't changed! When we can recognize these methods, and wisely choose to walk in love and keep our peace, we will walk in triumph in every circumstance we face! We don't have to take the bait!

The Holy Spirit Speed Bump

> But when He, the Spirit of truth, comes, He will guide you into all the truth; for He will not speak on His own initiative, but whatever He hears, He will speak; and He will disclose to you what is to come. John 16:13 (NASB)

> For the love of Christ constraineth us; 2 Corinthians 5:14a (KJV)

If we will listen to the Holy Spirit in our lives, He will give us a nudge when we are about to fall for the schemes of the enemy. Greg and I call this the "Holy Spirit Speed Bump" because it feels kind of like you are getting some resistance, as if the air just got thicker, but you can push through it, just like a speed bump when you are driving a car. As we started learning what peace felt like in our lives, when we messed up, we could go back and recall a "yellow light" feeling or an inward urging in our spirits, that we should have slowed down and stopped saying or thinking anything further. The Holy Spirit is a gentleman and will not force you to comply, but DO IT! He is trying to keep you out of trouble and out of strife! We began to pay attention to these speed bumps before continuing on and it really helped us avoid the pitfalls we had previously been falling into! Praise God, He loves us and has given us the Holy Spirit to help us succeed! —Sharon

What do we mean by "bait"?

Just like a fisherman uses a plethora of baits to catch various types of fish, so too our enemy has crafted some special lures just for us, to catch us unaware and deceive us. We have identified these nine specific "lures" in the Word of God and we have seen in our lives how the enemy uses them to steal our peace:

Jealousy

For wherever there is jealousy (envy) and contention (rivalry and selfish ambition), there will also be confusion (unrest, disharmony, rebellion) and all sorts of evil and vile practices. James 3:16 (AMP)

Unforgiveness

And be kind to one another, tenderhearted, forgiving one another, even as God in Christ forgave you. Ephesians 4:32 (NKJV)

Taking Offense over a perceived wrong

*[Love] does not act unbecomingly; it does not seek its own,
is not provoked, does not take into account a wrong suffered,
1 Corinthians 13:5 (NASB)*

Worry and Self-care

*Therefore humble yourselves under the mighty hand of God,
that He may exalt you in due time, casting all your care upon Him,
for He cares for you. 1 Peter 5:6-7 (NKJV)*

Criticism

*Do not speak against one another, brethren. He who speaks against
a brother or judges his brother, speaks against the law and judges
the law; but if you judge the law, you are not a doer of the law but a
judge of it. James 4:11 (NASB)*

Gossip

*Let no corrupt word proceed out of your mouth, but what is good
for necessary edification, that it may impart grace to the hearers.
Ephesians 4:29 (NKJV)*

Talebearing

*Where there is no wood, the fire goes out; And where there is no
talebearer, strife ceases. Proverbs 26:20 (NKJV)*

Judgment

*There is one Lawgiver, who is able to save and to destroy. Who are
you to judge another? James 4:12 (NKJV)*

Debate

*Remind them of these things, and solemnly charge them in the
presence of God not to wrangle about words, which is useless and leads
to the ruin of the hearers. Be diligent to present yourself approved
to God as a workman who does not need to be ashamed, accurately
handling the word of truth. But avoid worldly and empty chatter,
for it will lead to further ungodliness, and their talk will spread like
gangrene. 2 Timothy 2:14–17a (NASB)*

When we begin to sense a lack of peace or see the signs of strife in our lives
somewhere, we can usually trace it back to a specific moment when we chose to
engage in one of those behaviors.

Paul charges us to

*Be sober, be vigilant; because your adversary the devil walks about
like a roaring lion, seeking whom he may devour. 1 Peter 5:8 (NKJV)*

And also,

*Be angry, and yet do not sin; do not let the sun go down on your anger,
and do not give the devil an opportunity. Ephesians 4:26–27 (NASB)*

As we start to recognize the schemes of the devil and the baits he is using in our
lives to get us out of peace and into strife, we need to remember what God's will for
us looks like. Reminding ourselves of God's Best for us will help us be willing to pay
the price it costs our flesh to submit to God and resist the devil! "Normal" for the
believer is a life filled with the glory and presence of God! He has promised us His
help in every area of need (Hebrews 4:16)! He has provided us His sweet presence
to guide us (Hebrews 13:5) and His power to strengthen us (Phil. 4:13)! When we
realize what we would be giving up to wallow in criticism or judgment, or any of the
other areas mentioned, we find it easier to resist those temptations and not take
the bait!

When Joseph was tempted by his boss's wife to commit adultery in Genesis 39,
he answered in verse 9, "How then can I do this great wickedness, and sin against
God?" (NKJV). Joseph knew God's promises for his life, even though he didn't
see them yet. He was unwilling to give up God's best for him for the momentary

pleasures of sin. God honored that, and just a few years later, Joseph was second in command of all of Egypt! When we are so in love with God, His presence in our lives, and His best for us, the temptations of the enemy lose their allure in comparison to what we have gained in Christ. Knowing God's best for us helps us to remember, **"DON'T TAKE THE BAIT!"**

Questions

1. What are some characteristics of strife that you have seen in your own life?

_____

_____

_____

2. Think of a time this past week where you have gotten into conflict or strife with someone. Now that you know the "baits" that are used to get you into strife, are you able to recognize one of these as a contributing factor in your situation?

_____

_____

_____

3. Now, go further back than one week and consider another painful situation caused by strife. List out the possible baits involved in that situation.

_____

_____

_____

4. Can you recognize which baits the enemy uses most often in your life?

_____

_____

_____

HOW TO GET OUT OF STRIFE

It was for freedom that Christ set us free; therefore keep standing firm and do not be subject again to a yoke of slavery. Galatians 5:1 (NASB)

As Sharon and I learned about these different baits, it became very evident that just knowing what NOT to do wasn't enough. We had to start learning what TO do. The life of a believer isn't just one of meekness and civility, but one of power and influence. God didn't bridge time and space to make a way for you to have fellowship with Him just so you could be some weak and pathetic person. He has made you more than a conqueror (Romans 8:37) and wants you to take ground for Him and His kingdom with boldness and confidence (Matt. 11:12). This requires that you first cast off the bonds the enemy puts on you and what you willingly take on yourself. Getting out of strife and back in peace and love is step number one in becoming this person of strength and influence.
—Greg

VERY IMPORTANT!!!

How to Get Out of Strife

What do we do if we have ignored the Holy Spirit Speed Bump and find ourselves with a hook in our mouth? When we are out of the peace of God and in a strife-filled situation? This will happen to all of us from time to time, as long as we are on this earth and in our fallible, sinful human flesh. The question isn't "what do we do IF we fall into strife?" but rather, "what do we do WHEN we fall into strife?"

First of all, we must remember those in Christ have no condemnation,

> *There is therefore now no condemnation to those who are in Christ Jesus, who do not walk according to the flesh, but according to the Spirit. Romans 8:1 (NKJV)*

Jesus doesn't condemn us! In Hebrews we read,

> *For we do not have a High Priest who cannot sympathize with our weaknesses, but was in all points tempted as we are, yet without sin. Hebrews 4:15 (NKJV)*

Not only does He understand our weaknesses, but He sympathizes with us, and can show us the way out! Hallelujah! We find the road map for getting out of strife and back into the perfect peace of God in James 4:6b-7.

> *God resists the proud, but gives grace to the humble. Therefore submit to God. Resist the devil and he will flee from you. (NKJV)*

So let's break this down into three steps:

#1 - **"Submit to God."** Humble yourself before God, confess your sins and repent of whatever bait you fell for. It might be that you were critical of someone, or judged someone's motives. Whatever the case, it is very important that you are intellectually honest with God, yourself, and any others that may have been affected. We cannot over-stress this, because without total honesty and integrity, you will not have victory, because you are not truly subjected to God. Only through complete submission to God and His word will you have His power to resist the enemy.

If you are having trouble deciphering which bait you have taken, pray and ask God for help! He wants you to be free and walk in His freedom. Walking in the truth about our actions is part of that. It is humbling, but oh so powerful! When we choose to plow ahead with Step Two before we complete Step One, we won't be successful!

Here is an example prayer: "Lord, I'm sorry. I took a bait and I ... (insert bait here: criticized my boss, judged my spouse, debated politics with my brother, was jealous of my sister...) I repent. I change my mind on that and choose to think like You do about it. Please forgive me."

When you take this step to submit yourself to God, you are repositioning yourself back under His authority. With this authority, you will be able to take the next step of resisting the enemy.

#2 - **"Resist the devil."** Now that you have effectively gotten back under the umbrella of God's provision, you can drive the devil right out of your situation and life. This action can take many different forms, but the core of it is to stand up "inside" yourself and resist the enemy (Ephesians 6:13). Imagine if someone came up to you and started attacking you. You wouldn't just stand there and take it, you would start fighting back! Resistance means to come against, to push back. In Step One, you have repented of taking the bait. You are now forgiven, in perfect standing with God, and have access to the power of God. Take that power and aim it at the devil by saying "Satan, get away from me, I am forgiven!" Proclaim that the enemy cannot be near you, your family, your job, etc... Be obstinate, get in his face! Resist! The act of verbally coming against the enemy is powerful and when you come against him after submitting yourself to God, he cannot ignore you!

1 Peter 5:9 states you are to

> *Resist him [the devil], steadfast in the faith, knowing that the same sufferings are experienced by your brotherhood in the world. (NKJV)*

#3 - **Receive God's peace.** Lastly, begin verbally thanking God for His Word and that when you submit to Him and resist the enemy, that the devil must go away. This is the final action of total submission to the belief that God is in charge and able to keep his children in the perfect peace that Jesus walked in on the Earth (John 14:27).

An example would sound like this: "I thank You Lord that Your Word is true and that as I submit to You and resist the devil, he HAS to flee from me! I also thank You for Your peace that was given to me in Christ. You are always with me. Thank You!"

These steps may seem unnatural and even weird, but they will absolutely work when we are humble before God. We need to remember:

> *For we do not wrestle against flesh and blood, but against principalities, against powers, against the rulers of the darkness of this age, against spiritual hosts of wickedness in the heavenly places. Ephesians 6:12 (NKJV)*

Our battle is not against flesh and blood. Taking authority over the enemy is an action we may never have done in our entire lives, but as born-again believers, it is an action we were created to make. Sometimes we can actually feel the peace of God descending on us, and it is an amazing sensation. But whether we feel any different or not, we know that the Word of God is true and works! We will find that peace and joy returns to our lives because He Who promised is faithful (Hebrews 10:23). Our "normal" will begin to change and become joyful, peaceful, victorious...LIFE!

Sometimes we have to repeat these steps a few times to catch every bait we may have taken. If we don't sense an immediate shift from strife to peace, we need to spend some more time with Jesus in prayer, seeking his perspective and wisdom about what's really going on. He wants us to have all He paid for us have. He wants us to walk in peace, always. Sometimes it just takes a shift in our thinking to submit to His will so we can receive it all.

As we continue to walk in Powerful Peace, the distance between times of strife will lengthen. We may start out having to confront strife every hour for a while, but then we will notice that it's been an entire afternoon that we've been enjoying sweet communion with the Lord. Then it will turn into a day or two, and suddenly we realize that our "normal" is being at peace with God, others, ourselves, and our circumstances. The strife that we lived with almost constantly, that robbed us of sleep, robbed us of God's peace, robbed us of health, etc. is not there any more. Now our "normal" is more like the "life, and life more abundantly" promised by our Lord Jesus Christ (John 10:10)!

I can positively say with all assurance that these steps to getting out of strife and back into God's peace work and work very well. This is because I can be somewhat of a knuckle-head and have had way too many opportunities to test them out. Hallelujah, God's Word works, and His mercies are renewed every morning! God continues to help me learn to stay in peace and out of strife. I can be taught! I keep learning how valuable His best is and it really makes it easier to resist the baits that come at me. They just aren't worth the price you pay. God's best is so much better than the opportunity to criticize or judge someone. —Greg

1. Why should you get out of strife?

_____

_____

_____

_____

2. Can you recognize which baits the enemy uses most often in your life?

_____

_____

_____

_____

3. What are the Three Steps you take to get out of strife? Give an explanation of each.

_____

_____

_____

_____

SPIRIT, SOUL, AND BODY

Now may the God of peace Himself sanctify you entirely; and may
your spirit and soul and body be preserved complete, without blame at
the coming of our Lord Jesus Christ.
1 Thessalonians 5:23 (NASB)

In order for us to understand how the baits of the enemy are able to tempt us, we first need to understand how we relate to God and the world now that we are new in Christ. God created humanity in His image and just as God is three in one, so are we. It is His will that all three—spirit, soul, and body—be "preserved complete, without blame" when Jesus appears again. That means He wants us to walk in victory in every area of our existence on earth while we are here. Learning about these different areas in our lives will help us to do just that!

We are a spirit. We have a soul. We live in a body.

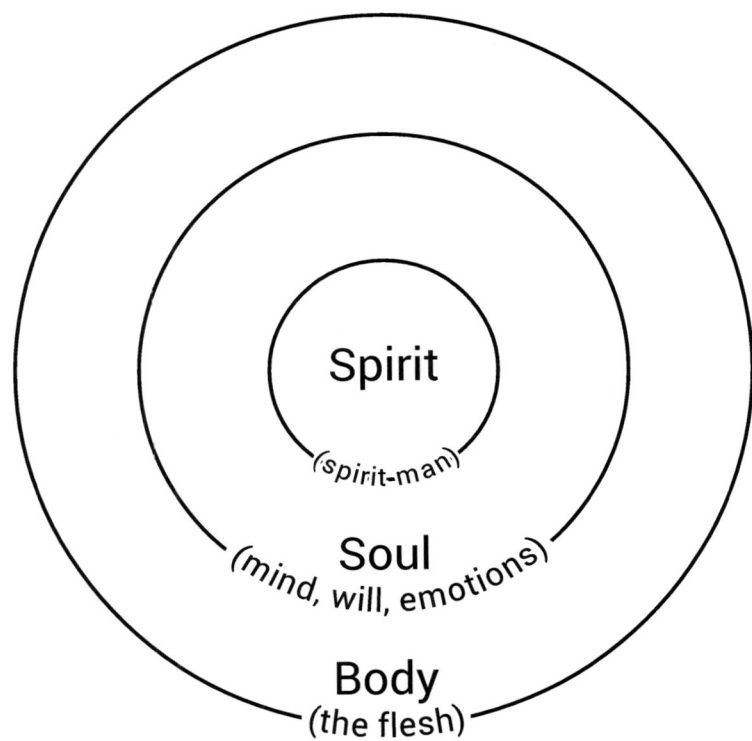

We are a spirit

Our spirit is the part of us that is our true nature, our true selves in Christ and the part of us that is eternal. It is also known as our "heart". Our spirits were the part of us that was dead from birth because of sin (Ephesians 2:1-3), but is reborn and "resurrected" when we receive Christ as our Lord and Savior (Ephesians 2:4-5). In John 3, Jesus tells Nicodemus that he must be "born again" (John 3:3), and then explains,

> *"Truly, truly, I say to you, unless one is born of water and the Spirit he cannot enter into the kingdom of God. That which is born of the flesh is flesh, and that which is born of the Spirit is spirit." John 3:5-6 (NASB)*

This was hard for Nicodemus to comprehend and receive because the idea of a spiritually dead Jew was a foreign concept to him. The Jews had been given special status with God as His chosen people, so to imply that they were still dead in their sins under the old covenant was an alien concept, and caused many of the Jewish leaders to stumble over Jesus's words. Jesus was trying to convey to Nicodemus the new birth experience of salvation by using the imagery of human birth. Jesus was illustrating that when one becomes "born again,"(another phrase used for salvation by grace through faith), his spirit is reborn, brand new. This is such good news for us because there are some really amazing characteristics of a brand new spirit!

Our spirit is a brand new creature in Christ.

Therefore if anyone is in Christ, he is a new creature; the old things passed away; behold, new things have come. 2 Corinthians 5:17 (NASB)

The desires of our heart have completely changed. The old things we wanted have passed away, and new things have come! God has taken out our old, dead-to-God, spirit, and replaced it with a new spirit that loves Him and wants to please Him always. We will find this so incredibly helpful as we grow into the maturity of Jesus Christ Himself. It is no coincidence that when God places His Holy Spirit within us at salvation, it is called the "seed" of the Holy Spirit. God comes to live within our hearts by His Spirit; His love, His character, and His righteousness start to germinate in the rich soil of our new spirits in Christ. As we yield to His Spirit's directions, we grow, flourish, and bear fruit!

Our new creation spirit wants to please and obey God in all things! Paul writes,

For you have not received a spirit of slavery leading to fear again, but you have received a spirit of adoption as sons by which we cry out, "Abba! Father!" Romans 8:15 (NASB)

And as His children, it is our delight to be with Him and love Him with our words, our attitudes, and our actions.

If you have never received Christ as your savior, there is a prayer on page … that you can pray to become born again and receive the Holy Spirit!

Our spirits cannot sin.

No one who is born of God practices sin, because His seed abides in
him; and he cannot sin, because he is born of God. 1 John 3:9 (NASB)

Another great characteristic of our new spirit in Christ is that because we are now born of God, our nature isn't a sin nature any longer. Our spirit, being born of God, wants to act like Him and please Him in all things. If we, after being saved, have ever watched a sinful TV show that we used to watch all the time before, you will notice the vast difference in our attitudes about it. Movies that used to never prick our conscience in any way before we met Jesus may now grieve our heart, or even make us feel physically ill. This is encouraging, and show us how our spirits are brand-new upon salvation. It's an amazing thing and we walk in abundant joy and peace as we yield to the Holy Spirit's gentle nudging to follow Jesus in our lives.

Our spirits are in constant contact with God.

The spirit of man is the lamp of the Lord,
Searching all the innermost parts of his being. Proverbs 20:27 (NASB)

Our spirits are where God speaks to us. Because God is spirit, we communicate with Him using our new spirits. We hear His voice speak to us, quietly and gently, as we spend time in prayer with Him. His Spirit shines on His Word as we spend time reading the Bible and we can understand what it means. And in reflective moments of self doubt, trouble, pain, or confusion, He reminds us that we are His children, holy and dearly loved:

For you have not received a spirit of slavery leading to fear again,
but you have received a spirit of adoption as sons by which we cry out,
"Abba! Father!" The Spirit Himself testifies with our spirit that we
are children of God. Romans 8:16 (NASB)

Our new nature in Christ doesn't languish in slavish fear for the present or the future any longer, but we cry out to our mighty Father God for help and protection. He truly has given us everything we need for life and Godliness (2 Peter 1:3), we must only press in to His love and grace for us!

New Believer

Spiritman made alive in Christ
Receives the seed of the Holy Spirit

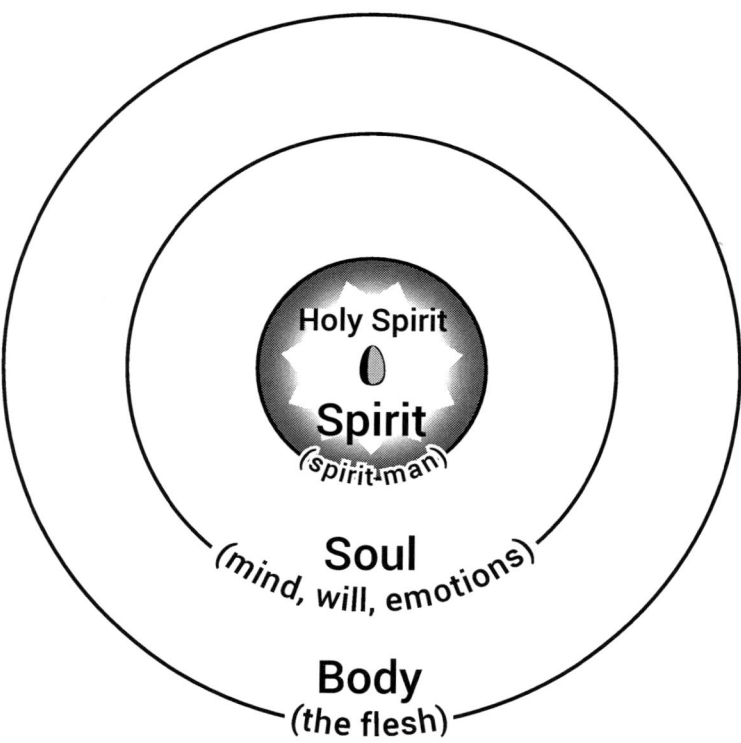

We have a soul

Our soul is the part of us also known as our mind, our will, and our emotions. This is the part of us that reasons, feels, decides, and thinks.

Our mind is part of our soul.

How our minds think is entirely up to us. This part becomes more and more like Christ as we renew our minds in the Word of God. The process whereby we mature in our ability to outwardly express the righteousness we received by faith when we were saved is called "sanctification." This is just a fancy word for maturing in our Christian behavior and it is the natural by-product of spending time with Christ and His Word, receiving God's will as our final authority in all things.

> *And do not be conformed to this world, but be transformed by the renewing of your mind, so that you may prove what the will of God is, that which is good and acceptable and perfect. Romans 12:2 (NASB)*

God wants to bless us and those around us with His will, which is good and acceptable and perfect. This doesn't happen effectively when our thinking is still polluted by sin and the world. When we replace the worldly, culturally-bankrupt thinking we had before our salvation with Godly, kingdom-thinking and believing, our behavior naturally follows.

For instance, before salvation, we may have habitually lied about a coworker in order to make our own reputation better. We may have taken credit for their work, or purposefully sabotaged their efforts out of jealousy. But after salvation, our desires change. We honestly begin to love this other person and want what's best for them. The Holy Spirit leads us to 1 Corinthians 13 which states,

> *Love is kind and is not jealous...*

Now, we find ourselves agreeing with Him and desiring to follow His example in our workplace. Jesus paid for all of our sins of lying and jealousy, but now that behavior grieves the Holy Spirit in our hearts and we want to stop it. As we submit to Him and confess our sin before Him, agreeing that it's wrong and that we don't want to do it anymore, His forgiveness heals our hearts and gives us the strength to love instead.

If we will listen intently to the Holy Spirit, the Spirit of truth, He will lead us into all truth (John 16:13). But in order for us to walk in those things, we have to receive them first by receiving His Word implanted in our souls. Our old thinking must be renovated—we must be renewed in our minds. We must use our will, on purpose, to agree with what God says.

Our will is part of our soul.

When we became a Christian, we made a decision. We listened to a preacher or a teacher or a parent share with us the wonderful Gospel of Jesus Christ, and we were convicted by the Holy Spirit of our own personal need for salvation. We received the truth and acted on it, on purpose. Now, we most assuredly didn't understand the full ramifications of that decision at that time, and the abundance we would inherit through Christ, but on a conscious level, we chose Jesus. God so values our willful choice to respond to His goodness toward us in Christ, that He will not violate our ability to choose, even if it means we choose to reject His most precious gift and end up spending eternity in Hell, separated from His loving presence forever. Our will is sacred to Him and He will not infringe on our right to make our own decisions. But He will always be there to encourage us to make good, fruitful decisions! A favorite scripture that illustrates this is found in Deuteronomy 30:19,

> *I call heaven and earth to witness against you today, that I have set before you life and death, the blessing and the curse. So choose life in order that you may live, you and your descendants. (NASB)*

Here, God is encouraging the nation of Israel to follow His ways so that He can prosper them. You can clearly see how He is showing them that they have a choice, "I have set before you life and death, the blessing and the curse..." but He is also giving them the answer to the test with "so choose life in order that you may live..."!

This freedom to choose is why we need to renew our minds with the Word of God. We can't made good decisions when our beliefs aren't based on the truth. What we believe will ultimately determine what we can receive from God. If we don't believe He loves us, it is exceedingly hard to receive His blessings or to even recognize them when they come to us. Thankfully, He knows it is hard to change our thinking and our believing, so He shows us in His Word how to affect change in our minds, and ultimately our wills. James 1:21 says,

> *Therefore, putting aside all filthiness and all that remains of wickedness, in humility receive the word implanted, which is able to save your souls. (NASB)*

The Greek word here for "save" is "*soh-dzo*" which also means to deliver out of danger and into safety, to restore, to preserve, and to make well. You see, your spirit man was made immediately perfect in Christ at salvation, but our mind, our will, and our emotions take some time to transition from the old man to the new man. We can see from James that we do this by humbly receiving the Word of God, and His powerful Word will transform us from the inside out! We must acknowledge that His Word is the truth—the final authority in our lives—whether we understand it or agree with it or not. Then we must choose to submit to it, receiving all that He shows us through the Holy Spirit.

Our emotions are part of our soul.

There are so many emotions we can have on any given day! We can be feeling on top of the world in the morning, but by lunchtime be down in the dumps, then rebound by dinner when we have a great time with friends over pizza! So many waves, it can be daunting to try and navigate the good ones while avoiding the bad ones.

Our emotions are a gift from God and are to be used by us as an indicator of our spiritual and mental states. Emotions are like a thermometer because they demonstrate the temperature of the surrounding area, or the belief system upon which they are founded. We can use this fact to our advantage by digging a little deeper. Because our emotions stem from what we believe, we will have pleasant, peaceful emotions when we are believing the truth, and we will have unpleasant, even disturbing emotions when we are meditating on anything other than the truth. Paul illustrates this fact in Romans 8:6,

> *For the mind set on the flesh is death, but the mind set on the Spirit is life and peace. (NASB)*

Thoughts of God's love for us, of His provision, and of His mercy and grace that superabound toward us in Christ will overwhelm the thoughts and fears the enemy tries to bombard us with. When we encounter those crippling fears, anxious thoughts, and condemning voices, we can simply turn our attention away from those lying voices and meditate on who He is, what He has done, and what He has said to us in His Word. So when we find ourselves struggling with any negative emotions, we need to stop and dig a little deeper to find out what thought or belief these feelings are the fruit of. And as we choose to sow the Word of God into our souls, we will find ourselves spontaneously agreeing more and more with the way God thinks, believes, and acts.

For it is God who is at work in you, both to will and to
work for His good pleasure. Philippians 2:13 (NASB)

At first, as we begin renewing our minds with God's Word and walking in the Spirit instead of our old habits, it can feel unnatural. It can seem foolish to our unrenewed mind to trust in an invisible God and His Word and Spirit, but if we are willing to trust Him with our eternity, surely we can trust Him with our fleeting, earthly existence! He is so able to carry us through! And as we continue to lean on Him and His greater understanding, we find Him ever faithful and sure.

Growing Believer

Sanctification (cleansing) in progress
Rennovation of beliefs and values

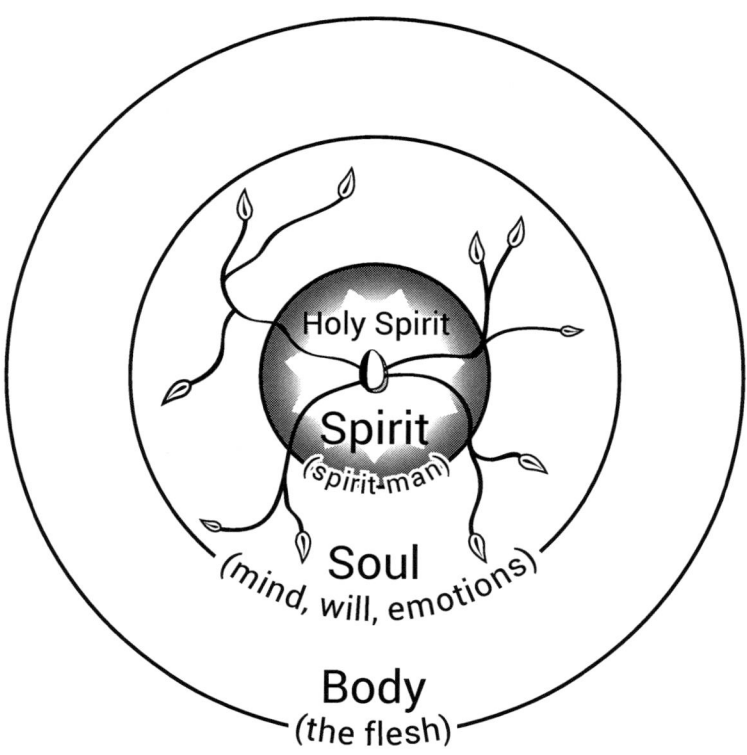

Holy Spirit

Spirit
(spirit-man)

Soul
(mind, will, emotions)

Body
(the flesh)

When Sharon and I were first learning about strife and walking in peace, we had been having trouble with being consistent. God gave me some revelation about the natural state of things. He gave me a vision of a wheel that was spinning. It was similar to a bicycle wheel and it would just automatically start spinning with no help from anyone. God explained to me that this was representative of the fallen world we live in and that if we do nothing the wheel of life will spin, but in the wrong direction (James 3:6). God wants us to stop the wheel and spin it the other direction! (Ephesians 5:15-16)

When we choose to ignore God's Word or the direction of the Holy Ghost, the wheel will automatically spin the wrong direction. What happens when the wheel spins the wrong direction? All the bad things happen, including strife, arguments, poverty, separation in relationships, attacks from the enemy, etc... How do we stop the wheel and spin it the right direction? Wake up! Choose on purpose to not just go along with what's going on around you. Then choose to establish God's righteousness (His way of doing and being right) into your situation by doing the right thing. For me, it was to choose not to argue. There were many times I just bit my lip and said no more. Then I would go out of my way to bless Sharon and do things I knew she liked. This wasn't to stop the argument, but was based on a deeper motive of wanting God's best and to see His amazing hand at work. There is a huge difference between just sucking it up and taking it on the chin, and sowing seeds of peace.
—Greg

We live in a body

This part of us is also known as our flesh. This is the shell that houses our soul, our spirit, and the Holy Spirit. It's kind of like the house we live in now. We would never go to our neighbors empty house and start up a conversation about the weather, or the construction going on at the end of our street. That would be absurd because we know the house is not the family that lives there. Our bodies are the same thing for us. Remember, we ARE a spirit, we HAVE a soul, and we LIVE in a body.

Our body is not the REAL us.

Our bodies are just the temporary dwelling place for our soul and our spirits. When our body dies, the real us will continue on with God in Heaven because of Christ. We will get a new body that doesn't decay and die. Hallelujah! The body of this flesh has been contaminated by sin and we wouldn't want to live in it forever anyway. Now because our flesh inherited a sin nature from our parents—everyone has because of Adam's sin—we can't lean on our flesh for any truth or goodness.

Our body is where fleshly, sinful desires originate.

> *Now the deeds of the flesh are evident, which are: immorality, impurity, sensuality, idolatry, sorcery, enmities, strife, jealousy, outbursts of anger, disputes, dissensions, factions, envying, drunkenness, carousing, and things like these, of which I forewarn you, just as I have forewarned you, that those who practice such things will not inherit the kingdom of God. Galatians 5:19-21 (NASB)*

Because our flesh is so greatly influenced by sin, we have to do something with it in order to live a victorious Christian life. We can't let our bodies rule us in any way.

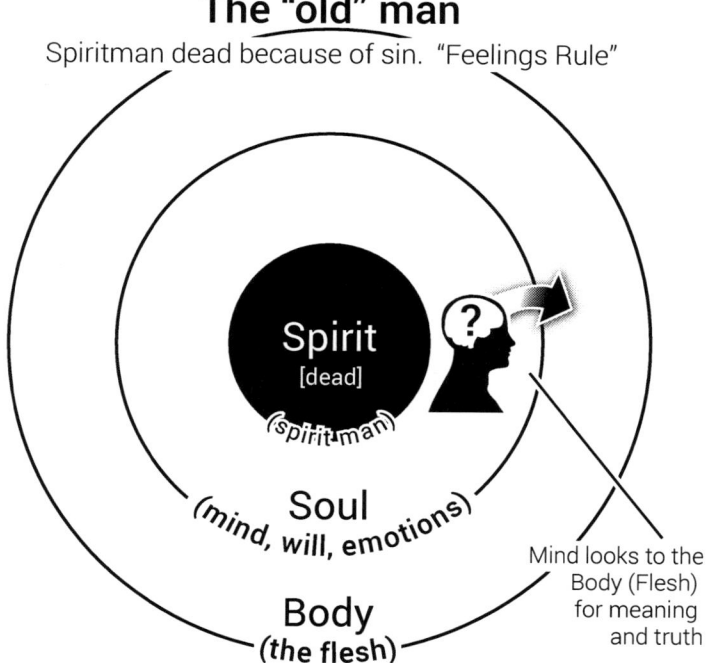

The "old" man
Spiritman dead because of sin. "Feelings Rule"

Spirit
[dead]
(spiritman)

Soul
(mind, will, emotions)

Body
(the flesh)

Mind looks to the Body (Flesh) for meaning and truth

We have to do something with our flesh.

We discovered earlier that we can renovate our souls by renewing our minds with God's Word, but the flesh isn't so workable. The fingerprint of sin goes all the way down to the molecular level, and it has to be continually denied, put down, and subjugated to our new spirit's desires and the Holy Spirit. Romans 12:1 illustrates it like this:

Therefore I urge you, brethren, by the mercies of God, to present your bodies a living and holy sacrifice, acceptable to God, which is your spiritual service of worship. (NASB)

Because of God's great mercies toward us in Christ, He has made us holy and acceptable. Our part is to present our bodies to God in obedience for His service.

Paul says even he has to

...keep under my body, and bring it into subjection: lest that by any means, when I have preached to others, I myself should be a castaway. 1 Corinthians 9:27 (KJV)

He shows us here that he makes a distinction between himself and his body. He considers these two different, separate entities and treats his body/flesh harshly; literally it says he "bruises" his body, to keep it in subjection to his spirit man. He is in no way advocating self harm in any way, but he is showing us the principle that he must rule his unruly fleshly desires and make himself do what his flesh doesn't want to do. The flesh is unable to do so (Romans 8:7) on its own, so relying on our it for any sort of wisdom or guidance is a sure way to go downhill!

The flesh has no more power over the believer.

Before salvation, we all were in bondage to a sinful nature and had no power within ourselves to resist its power to disrupt our relationships, cause chaos in our homes, and inflict others with our selfishness or pride. But now, because we have been identified with Christ through His crucifixion and resurrection, our flesh has been crucified as well. We have been set free from the power of sin in our lives, no longer forced to obey its lusts, and are free to walk in the new desires and characteristics of our Heavenly Father. Consider the following scriptures:

Even so consider yourselves to be dead to sin, but alive to God in Christ Jesus. Romans 6:11 (NASB)

Now those who belong to Christ Jesus have crucified the flesh with its passions and desires. Galatians 5:24 (NASB)

Now, read them again, paying attention to the verb tenses in each verse.

They are past tense, right? This has already taken place, it just takes our flesh time to catch on! Before we become Christians, we are ruled by our fleshly desires and carnal thinking. When we become a Christian, only our spirit is recreated in Christ. Our body and soul must be put under subjection to the Word, the Holy Spirit, and our new recreated spirits.

Mature Believer

Stable, secure, productive, fruitful

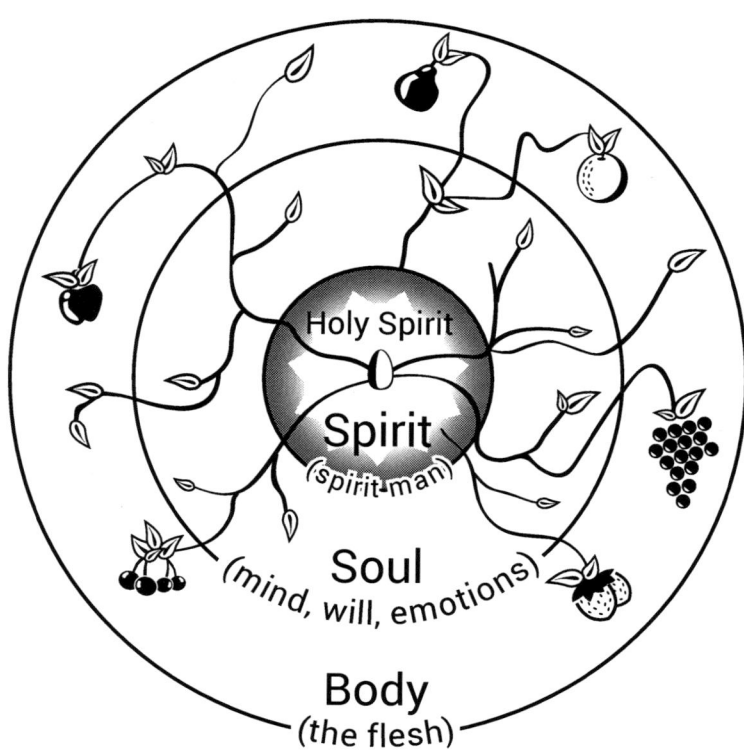

Powerful Peace will walk us through nine specific areas that Christians struggle with and explain how to walk in victory. As we uncover who we are in Christ and agree with the Holy Spirit as He shows us His will for us, these baits will stop working in our lives and we will start producing more and more fruit in every area.

Why This Matters

The baits used by the enemy work by tempting either the areas of our soul that are unrenewed, or the areas where we allow our flesh to reign. Either way, these nine areas simply show us where we are not walking in the fullness of who we are in Christ. They are never meant to be a source of self-condemnation, but simply an area that God wants us to mature in and receive all we have inherited in Christ. We need to remember that our body is not the "real us," and its desires are contrary to God's desires (Romans 8:7). It is merely the vessel in which our spirit resides. Our soul is not the "real us" either, and can be controlled by either the world or the Holy Spirit, depending on whether we renew our minds with the Word of God or not. When we renew our thinking with the Word of God, and remember that we are "dead to sin and alive to God in Christ Jesus" (Romans 6:11), we won't be derailed in our growth and maturity!

Questions:

1. Knowing that self-control is a fruit of the spirit, how does this scripture illustrate the difference between our spirit and our body?

_____

_____

_____

_____

A person without self-control is like a city with broken-down walls.
Proverbs 25:28 (NLT)

2. In what areas of your life do you see the need to renew your mind as in Romans 12:2?

_____

_____

_____

_____

3. In what areas of your life do you see the need to present your body to God as in Romans 12:1?

_____

_____

_____

WORKING VS BEARING

In chapter 5, we discovered that we are more than just what we think or how we feel. We are a multi-faceted creature that is an eternal spirit, has a soul, and lives in a body. Knowing this helps us to better manage ourselves and separate what God is telling our spirits from the facts in our minds or the emotions we feel. This helps us walk in victory in our lives instead of feeling doomed by our circumstances or dysfunctional relationships.

We have expounded on the unique characteristics of humanity in that we are a spirit, we have a soul, and we live in a body. Let's take a closer look at the differences that are found between the believing, spirit-led Christian and the one that hasn't yet taken this step of faith.

The flesh is in bondage

Before our salvation, we were prisoners to the sin found in our souls, minds, and flesh. Because we weren't born sinless, we never made a conscious decision to start sinning—it just happened. Before we could even speak a word, our selfish desires had taken over and we were demanding to be fed, changed, burped, and loved at all hours of the day and night. (Sorry Mom!) And to be honest, before Christ, we had no true free will—no choice on whether to blame others for our sin, no choice on whether to sin or not—we sinned because we were sinners. We sinned because we were alive to sin, drawing our desires, understanding, and choices from our sinful nature. We were dead to God, not caring about what He wanted at all. Paul shows the difference between believers (Christians) and non-believers (Gentiles) in Ephesians 4,

With the Lord's authority I say this: Live no longer as the Gentiles do, for they are hopelessly confused. Their minds are full of darkness; they wander far from the life God gives because they have closed their minds and hardened their hearts against him. They have no sense of shame. They live for lustful pleasure and eagerly practice every kind of impurity. Ephesians 4:17-19 (NLT)

The law was only able to *curb* the sinful behavior, but could never actually *prevent* the works of the flesh from contaminating our lives and the lives of those around us. Eventually, our self-determination to be righteous burns out as our willpower fails. The nine baits we will be discussing in later chapters come from our old, unregenerated, and sinful flesh and mind—our old natures apart from Christ.

Paul illustrates this principle in Galatians 5 and helps us identify the works of the flesh.

Now the deeds of the flesh are evident, which are:
immorality, impurity, sensuality, idolatry, sorcery,
enmities, strife, jealousy, outbursts of anger, disputes,
dissensions, factions, envying, drunkenness, carousing, and things like
these, of which I forewarn you, just as I have forewarned you, that
those who practice such things will not inherit the kingdom of God.
Galatians 5:19-21 (NASB)]

The illustration on the next page shares how this works in our lives. Anyone who has ever cut a lawn knows that dandilions are impossible to get rid of by simply cutting them with a lawn mower. The head and its seeds keep growing back. This is because you never address the root of the weed.

God sent mankind the law to show him his need for a Savior. Unfortunately, mankind started trying to use the law as a means to obtain self righteousness by keeping it. This just made sin stronger in the flesh and mankind's behavior raged against the law that was holding evil behavior at bay. The law had no power in itself to actually cure man of sin. It seeks to cut off or hide the evil behavior, but the root cause of sin remains and continues to bear evil seeds day after day, season after season, year after year.

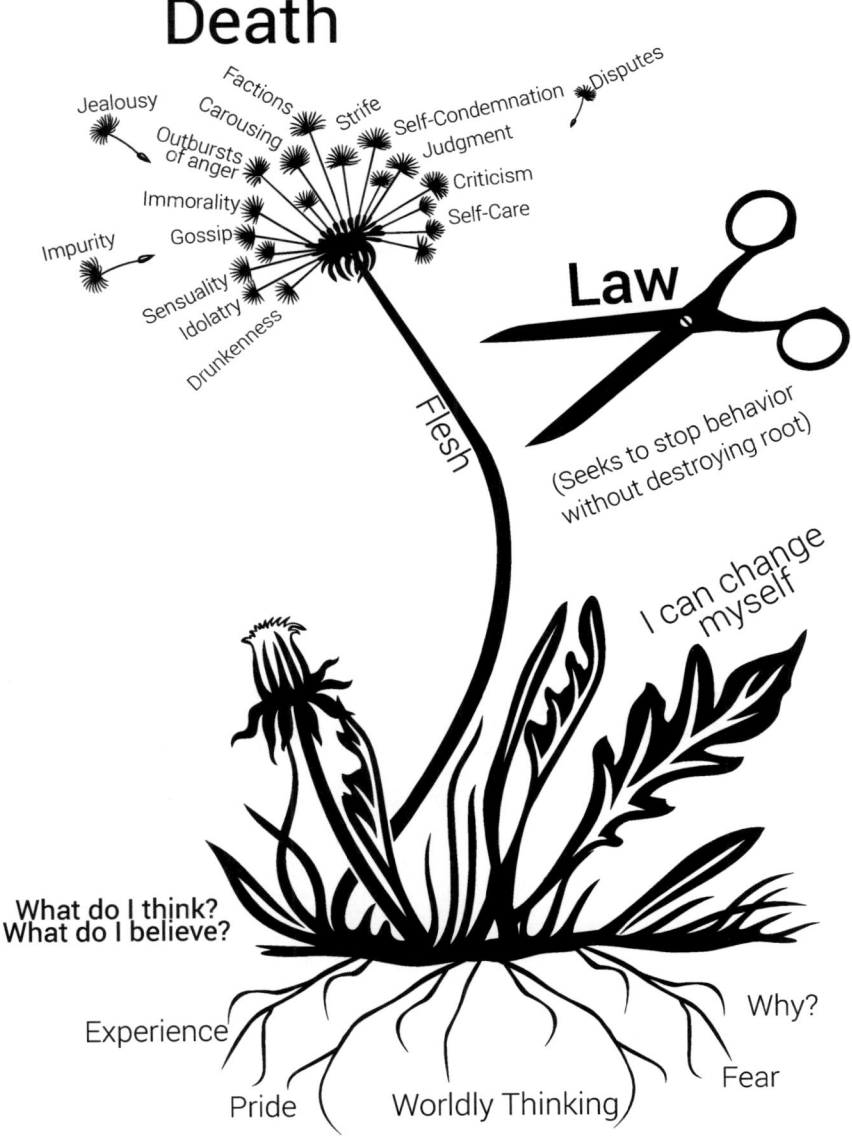

Death

Jealousy
Factions
Carousing
Strife
Self-Condemnation
Disputes
Outbursts of anger
Judgment
Immorality
Criticism
Self-Care
Impurity
Gossip
Sensuality
Idolatry
Drunkenness

Flesh

Law

(Seeks to stop behavior
without destroying root)

I can change
myself

What do I think?
What do I believe?

Experience

Why?

Pride

Worldly Thinking

Fear

I remember as a child having so much fun picking dandelion heads and blowing them into the wind, completely oblivious to the fact that I was spreading these weed-making seeds all over our neighborhood! Our kids also enjoyed doing this when a stray dandelion would rear its ugly head in our front yard as well. And let's face it, it's fun! But just like this illustration shows, these fleshly behaviors can sow seeds of doubt, anger, and strife into our own lives and the lives of others around us. Although the law is able to help us recognize these offensive tendencies, it has no real power in itself to change the plants that produce these seeds.
—Sharon

God's will for us to be completely free from the influence of the old man, and submitted completely to our new creation spirit in Christ. It looks a lot better on us!

> But the fruit of the Spirit is love, joy, peace, patience, kindness, goodness, faithfulness, gentleness, self-control; against such things there is no law. Galatians 5:22-23 (NASB)]

There is no law needed to curb the fruit of the Spirit in Christ Jesus, because we will always produce good fruit as we abide in Him. The old life without Christ was terrible, but praise be to God for our new life in Christ! Because of Him, we are now alive to God and dead to sin and its ability to force us to submit to its desires and thus produce sin and death in our lives. Now because we are born-again in spirit, we have God's strength within us to be the new creature He created us to be. We are truly free to choose what to obey—our Loving Father or our fleshly desires.

Walking in the Spirit

So how do we do this? How can we practically turn away from our old selves and embrace the newness of our spirits and have all that God wants for us?

> But I say, walk by the Spirit, and you will not carry out the desire of the flesh. - Galatians 5:16 (NASB)

> If we live by the Spirit, let us also walk by the Spirit. Galatians 5:23 (NASB)

LIFE

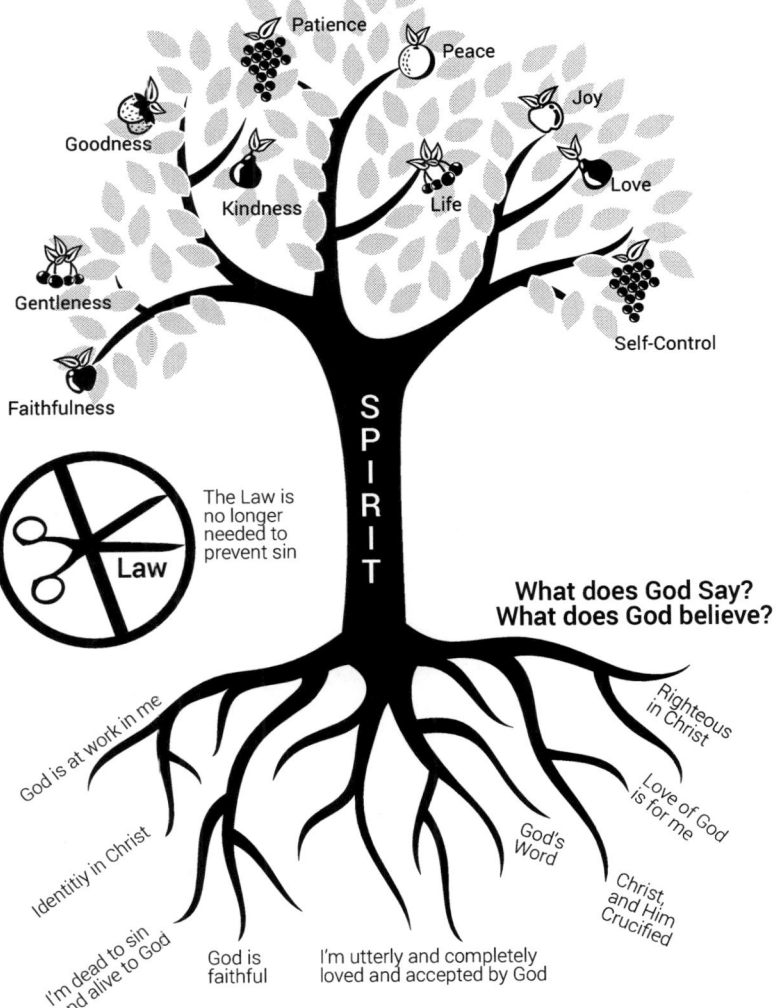

Patience

Peace

Joy

Goodness

Kindness

Life

Love

Gentleness

Self-Control

Faithfulness

S
P
I
R
I
T

Law

The Law is
no longer
needed to
prevent sin

What does God Say?
What does God believe?

God is at work in me

Righteous
in Christ

Identitiy in Christ

Love of God
is for me

God's
Word

I'm dead to sin
and alive to God

Christ,
and Him
Crucified

God is
faithful

I'm utterly and completely
loved and accepted by God

God wants us to "walk in the Spirit" instead of letting our flesh take us where it wants. It is impossible for us to walk in the Spirit and walk in the flesh at the same time. God knows this, so He gave us the ability to focus on the stronger Spirit-led walk, which keeps us completely away from carrying out the desires of the flesh.

> *For those who are according to the flesh set their minds on the things of the flesh, but those who are according to the Spirit, the things of the Spirit. For the mind set on the flesh is death, but the mind set on the Spirit is life and peace, because the mind set on the flesh is hostile toward God; for it does not subject itself to the law of God, for it is not even able to do so, and those who are in the flesh cannot please God. - Romans 8: 5-8 (NASB)*

Why don't we just naturally walk in the gift of His peace from the get-go?

When we gave our lives to Christ, we were plucked out of our state of depravity and transformed instantly into children of God. In a flash, we were made righteous before God and could boldly approach Him with confidence. This sounds like the plot from an epic movie! So why do we still struggle to walk in His peace? Why doesn't it just happen? This is the million dollar question.

Because we have spent our lives trying to control our external, sinful behavior by rules and self-discipline, it is very easy and very natural for us to continue this tendency after our salvation. We are taught right from wrong and the Golden Rule from our youth, and we just keep this up as we try to mature in our relationship with God. What does Paul have to say about all this trying to do right in our own strength?

> *Let me ask you this one question: Did you receive the Holy Spirit by obeying the law of Moses? Of course not! You received the Spirit because you believed the message you heard about Christ. How foolish can you be? After starting your new lives in the Spirit, why are you now trying to become perfect by your own human effort? Have you experienced so much for nothing? Surely it was not in vain, was it? I ask you again, does God give you the Holy Spirit and work miracles among you because you obey the law? Of course not! It is because you believe the message you heard about Christ. - Galatians 3:2-5 (NLT)*

Paul is telling the Galatians, and us, that having begun in the spirit, in our hearts, we have to continue to grow and mature that same way. The greek word for "perfect" in verse 3 also means "mature." God wants us to grow in our maturity the same way we began our relationship with Him in the first place, by living out of our new created spirit in vital connection to Him and His Presence in us, trusting Him to work in and through us.

Jesus talks about this same growth in Him when He talks to his disciples during the Last Supper in John 15. This last meal He shared with His closest friends right before His crucifixion was full of His wisdom and instruction for us as His followers.

> *"I am the true vine, and My Father is the vinedresser. Every branch in Me that does not bear fruit, He takes away; and every branch that bears fruit, He prunes it so that it may bear more fruit. You are already clean because of the word which I have spoken to you. Abide in Me, and I in you. As the branch cannot bear fruit of itself unless it abides in the vine, so neither can you unless you abide in Me." John 15:1-4 (NASB)*

Abide

This means "to stay vitally connected to". Branches are so connected to the vines to which they belong, you can hardly see where one ends and the other begins. They look the same on the outside and the insides look similar as well. As long as this branch stays connected, it can ONLY grow and produce fruit! As a believer, if we will just remain in Him from the beginning to the end of our days, we will ONLY produce good fruit. This means to start our days thinking about Him and His words—reading the Bible, meditating on it, setting our imaginations in agreement with what He says about every circumstance and situation we come across during our days.

Jesus goes on to say in verse 5,

> *"I am the vine, you are the branches; he who abides in Me and I in him, he bears much fruit, for apart from Me you can do nothing."*

He is showing us that the only responsibility we have is to stay connected and abide in Him and allow Him to abide in us. If we will just do this, we will bear much fruit. But when we are trying to do these things—grow in faith, produce the fruit of the spirit, witness to others, share God's love—apart from our vital connection to Him and His Presence in us, we will fail. Our sinful flesh just can't do such things out of itself. The cool part is that He knows we can't do it on our own and He has no plans in requiring that of us! He has made allowance that we can do nothing without Him, so we don't have to!

1. Where are some areas in your life that you could benefit from abiding more in His Presence? Where could you use more fruit?

_____

_____

_____

Receive.

Something else we can notice as we look at the branch and vine illustration, is that the branch receives all it needs from the vine. Every grapevine branch draws all of its nutrition from the vine on which it grows. Healthy vines produce healthy branches! Healthy branches produce fruit! When we fail to see fruit on a healthy vine, we need to take a closer look at the branches. If the branches look damaged or sickly, it is always because something is blocking the vital sap from flowing to the branch. Either it has gotten twisted and bent, stopping the flow of water and nutrients, or it has been broken and separated from the vine altogether. This can happen in our lives as well. We won't flow in the peace and power of God in our lives if we don't receive His life-giving presence all the time, every day.

Paul told us that nothing could ever separate us from God's love for us and Jesus told us He would never leave us nor forsake us. There is never a separation between us and God in actuality, but sometimes we shut ourselves off from His presence. Because of sin in our lives, we may believe that He no longer loves us or no longer wants to spend time with us. Sometimes our feelings can reinforce these erroneous ideas, so we will act on that lie, further removing ourselves from Him and His people. Sometimes God asks us to do something we don't really want to do, so we run away from His presence, like Jonah. Whatever the reason, it is never God's will for us.

2. What are some reasons you aren't receiving from God? Where have you allowed your branch to become separated from Jesus—your vine?

_____

_____

_____

Rest.

Another curious thing we can learn from branches and vines, is that the branch doesn't have to strain and work at producing fruit if it is abiding in the vine and receiving its nutrition from the vine. Jesus said we will "bear much fruit" when we abide in Him. It's a done deal. We are designed by God to produce the fruit of the spirit when we abide in Him. We don't have to sweat it out; we don't have to "work it up." In fact, as we abide in Him, He is working in and through us. Paul puts it this way in Philippians 2:12-13 (NASB),

> So then, my beloved, just as you have always obeyed, not as in
> my presence only, but now much more in my absence, work out
> your salvation with fear and trembling; for it is God who is at work
> in you, both to will and to work for His good pleasure.

Paul is sharing with us here a key component to the spirit-led life in Christ, that it is GOD who is working in us. The Classic Amplified Paraphrase says it this way:

> [Not in your own strength] for it is God Who is all the
> while effectually at work in you [energizing and creating in you
> the power and desire], both to will and to work for His good
> pleasure and satisfaction and delight.

As the Holy Spirit shows us things He wants to change in us—from the bad habit of lying, to adulterous thoughts, to gossip—He gives us the desire to do it His way, and the power to follow through with those desires. Our part in this divine exchange is just to agree with Him and rest in Him as He does the changing and working from the inside out. When a branch starts to produce fruit, the vitamins and building blocks required to produce that fruit comes from the inside of the branch as the vine supplies everything the branch needs. As God reveals these areas to us, we can either try harder—working in our own strength and failing time and again—or we can trust more—allowing His Holy Spirit to give us the desire and power to obey His will. It *seems* counterintuitive at first, and even uncomfortable and fruitless, to let God work in and through us instead of trying harder to work it up ourselves, but it really works! And all the while, as He is working in and through us, we are resting in Him and giving Him all the thanks and praise for His work in us.

As we continue to study walking in Powerful Peace, we will show you how this works practically in our lives on a daily basis and you will walk a victorious spirit-led life as you let Him flow through you!

3. In what areas of your life have you been *trying* to pursue sanctification (practical holiness) instead of *trusting* God to do it in you?

_____

_____

_____

Let's choose to change that today!

WALKING IN LOVE

Love never fails... 1 Corinthians 13:8 (NASB)

It is God's will that we receive eternal life through our life in Christ. He also wants us to walk in freedom and abundant life right here, right now, on earth (John 10:10). We have introduced the idea of living our lives based on the Holy Spirit and our new creation spirit, in chapters five and six when we talked about our spirit, our soul, and our body. In order for us to consistently lay hold of the victory we have in Christ, we must consistently live out of our new nature instead of our unrenewed minds and our flesh. Paul calls this "walking in the spirit" in the New Testament, and it is the way Jesus lived out His life every single day.

So, what does walking in our new nature in Christ—our spirit—look like? It looks a lot like Jesus; it looks a lot like love. Jesus says in Matthew 5:43-48,

> *"You have heard that it was said, 'You shall love your neighbor and hate your enemy.' But I say to you, love your enemies and pray for those who persecute you, so that you may be sons of your Father who is in heaven; for He causes His sun to rise on the evil and the good, and sends rain on the righteous and the unrighteous. For if you love those who love you, what reward do you have? Do not even the tax collectors do the same? If you greet only your brothers, what more are you doing than others? Do not even the Gentiles do the same? Therefore you are to be perfect, as your heavenly Father is perfect."*

Now, trying to follow these principles on our own is impossible. Remember, using the law to curb our sinful, or selfish behavior in our own strength is like trying to plug an extension cord into itself! There is just no power there. But God is so sure of HIS ability within us to walk in His character traits, that He doesn't change His desire to see us do it. You see, He has already walked in it all in Jesus as He walked on this earth as a man. He KNOWS His power is sufficient within us as well, to complete all He has for us to do, but only as we forsake the idea that WE have to do it, and completely abandon our hearts to HIS desire and ability at work within us. Paul further explains this in Philippians 2:13 when he says,

> *"So then, my beloved, just as you have always obeyed, not as in my presence only, but now much more in my absence, work out your salvation with fear and trembling;* **for it is God who is at work in you,** *both to will and to work for His good pleasure."*

God's Love in Us Fulfills God's Will for Us

So now our focus no longer needs to be on avoiding the baits of the enemy or the sins of the flesh, but on walking according to the Spirit of God and agreeing with what He says about us! What does this look like? Let's look closer at Galatians 5:14-23.

> *For the whole Law is fulfilled in one word, in the statement,*
> *"You shall love your neighbor as yourself." But if you bite and devour one another, take care that you are not consumed by one another. But I say, walk by the Spirit, and you will not carry out the desire of the flesh. For the flesh sets its desire against the Spirit, and the Spirit against the flesh; for these are in opposition to one another, so that you may not do the things that you please. But if you are led by the Spirit, you are not under the Law. Now the deeds of the flesh are evident, which are: immorality, impurity, sensuality, idolatry, sorcery, enmities, strife, jealousy, outbursts of anger, disputes, dissensions, factions, envying, drunkenness, carousing, and things like these, of which I forewarn you, just as I have forewarned you, that those who practice such things will not inherit the kingdom of God. But the fruit of the Spirit is love, joy, peace, patience, kindness, goodness, faithfulness, gentleness, self-control; against such things there is no law. (NASB)*

So we see that if we are believing what the Spirit says about us, we aren't going to obey the desires of the flesh. If we are led by the Spirit, we are not going to be under the Law any longer, either. Why is this? Because the fruit of the Spirit is more powerful than the dictates of the law. If we are producing the fruit of the Spirit, we won't break any law because love is one of the fruits and love fulfills the law.

In 2005, after hurricane Katrina devastated the coasts of Mississippi and Louisiana, I volunteered to go help with disaster recovery through an organization called Service International. We were sent to help people in New Orleans get out of their mold-infested homes. This required that we empty the house of all their possessions and "muck" the inside by tearing out the drywall, frames, doors, etc. so we could bleach the timbers and kill the mold that had grown as a result of the widespread flooding. Even though I enjoyed doing it, the work was very difficult and tedious. At one point, I was using a crowbar to try to remove some door casings and I was frustrated as I would try to pry the casing off the wall. It would just bend and snap back into place. After several failed attempts, the Holy Spirit told me to use my crowbar to pry against the door frame. I did and the casing just popped right off. The Holy Spirit then told me that the reason it popped right off was because I was leveraging the crowbar on the immovable door frame instead of my own strength. He told me that I was doing the same thing in my spiritual life by trying in my own strength to get the supernatural results I longed to see. He wanted me to start relying on His strength found in His promises, instead of my own, to receive what was in my heart. —Greg

Love Fulfills the Law

In the Bible, the term "the law" was referring to either the Ten Commandments, the first five books of the Old Testament (the Torah), or the rules written down by Moses, referring to sacrifices, feasts, and other aspects of daily Jewish living. For the purposes of this chapter, we are going to deal mainly with the ten commandments. As we continue on, we will see how walking in love actually causes us to fulfill these commands effortlessly. Paul says in Romans,

Owe nothing to anyone except to love one another; for he who loves his neighbor has fulfilled the law. For this, "You shall not commit adultery, You shall not murder, You shall not steal, You shall not covet," and if there is any other commandment, it is summed up in this saying, "You shall love your neighbor as yourself." Love does no wrong to a neighbor; therefore love is the fulfillment of the law. Romans 13:8-10 (NASB)

We can see from this, that as we are walking in love, we won't do anything that might cause our neighbors harm in any way. When we are walking in love with God, ourselves, our families—with anyone, we are going to fulfill the law to overflowing. Remember the story Jesus tells about what following the spirit of the law, rather than the letter of the law, would look like in Matthew 5?

"You have heard that it was said, 'An eye for an eye, and a tooth for a tooth.' But I say to you, do not resist an evil person; but whoever slaps you on your right cheek, turn the other to him also. If anyone wants to sue you and take your shirt, let him have your coat also. Whoever forces you to go one mile, go with him two. Give to him who asks of you, and do not turn away from him who wants to borrow from you. You have heard that it was said, 'You shall love your neighbor and hate your enemy.' But I say to you, love your enemies and pray for those who persecute you, so that you may be sons of your Father who is in heaven; for He causes His sun to rise on the evil and the good, and sends rain on the righteous and the unrighteous. For if you love those who love you, what reward do you have?" Matthew 5:38-46 (NASB)

In our fleshly natural state, this would be absolutely impossible! Trying would only lead to our frustration and anger. We would expect reciprocation for our good deeds done, and if none came we might give up or retaliate and lash out in unforgiveness or bitterness. But when we are allowing the Spirit of God to flow in us and through us (remember we are to abide in Him?), we find this easy to do.

Peace comes when we trust God

As we choose to walk in the spirit, we will encounter trouble, trials, and tribulations. But because of His love for us, we trust in God to make things right for us, so we don't have to worry or fret about how things are going to turn out.

But God, being rich in mercy, because of His great love with which
He loved us, even when we were dead in our transgressions, made us
alive together with Christ (by grace you have been saved) Ephesians
2:4-5 (NASB)

We don't have to try to make things fair for ourselves. We know that God loves us and is for us and will work all things out according to His good will and purposes for us.

And we know that God causes all things to work together for good to
those who love God, to those who are called according to His purpose.
Romans 8:28 (NASB)

When we hold these attitudes, we will find it so much easier to trust Him and to walk in love and peace with others. We know He is working all things together for our good. We lean into His powerful love for us, knowing He has only good purposes and plans for us. Even when our situations seem hard or impossible, we can trust He will lead us through it all, and we will come out unscathed on the other side.

Leaning on His Love

So, how do we know that we even have the ability to "walk in love"? Where does it come from?

Therefore, having been justified by faith, we have peace with God
through our Lord Jesus Christ, through whom also we have obtained
our introduction by faith into this grace in which we stand; and
we exult in hope of the glory of God. And not only this, but we also
exult in our tribulations, knowing that tribulation brings about
perseverance; and perseverance, proven character; and proven
*character, hope; and hope does not disappoint, **because the love of God***
***has been poured out within our hearts through the Holy Spirit** who*
was given to us. Romans 5:1-5 (NASB)

When we received the Holy Spirit from God as we received our salvation, something amazing was also deposited in our hearts at the same time—the Love of God! Let's think about this for just a moment. The love of God has been (past tense) poured out within our hearts through the Holy Spirit. The love of God is already there. His love that fulfills the law is already present in our hearts! Let's look at another scripture to see what God's love in us is capable of.

Love endures long and is patient and kind; love never is envious
nor boils over with jealousy, is not boastful or vainglorious, does
not display itself haughtily. It is not conceited (arrogant and
inflated with pride); it is not rude (unmannerly) and does not act
unbecomingly. Love (God's love in us) does not insist on its own
rights or its own way, for it is not self-seeking; it is not touchy or
fretful or resentful; it takes no account of the evil done to it [it pays
no attention to a suffered wrong]. It does not rejoice at injustice and
unrighteousness, but rejoices when right and truth prevail.
Love bears up under anything and everything that comes, is ever
ready to believe the best of every person, its hopes are fadeless under all
circumstances, and it endures everything [without weakening].
Love never fails [never fades out or becomes obsolete or comes to an
end]. 1 Corinthians 13:4-8 (AMP)

So, to walk in peace and victory we need to walk in the Spirit and in love. Because we have the Holy Spirit of God, the love of God, and the ability to express it in whatever situation we are in, is poured out in our hearts as well! Hallelujah!

Now, how does this affect our ability to walk in peace with others? Do we still need to be wary of the baits? How do we stay out of strife? Let's consider this... Are we going to be condemning our neighbors if we are walking in love? Since love does no wrong to a neighbor (Romans 13:10), we aren't going to judge or criticize our neighbor. Love will pray for a neighbor. Love will call a neighbor up and ask if they need help when they fall off their ladder and break an elbow. Love doesn't even consider gossiping about the neighbor to others, but wants to protect their reputation because love does no wrong to a neighbor. When we are walking in the love of God, the powerful peace of God comes naturally and the baits seem absolutely absurd!

God's love within us is already prepared to answer when we encounter various temptations during our daily lives. All we need to do is yield to the Holy Spirit within us and let His love flow to ourselves and those around us. When one of the enemy's baits is presented to us, we can just simply turn to the love of God that is already poured out within our hearts, and answer the bait with God's love. When we are tempted to criticize our spouse for becoming angry with us for something we didn't do, we can look to the love of God already in our hearts, and forgive and bless them instead of needing to defend ourselves. When our children interrupt us for the tenth time while we are watching a movie and they should already be asleep, we can look to the love of God in our hearts and forgive them and tuck them in with a kiss and a prayer. You see, the love of God in us is patient and kind, so we can be patient and kind to others as we yield to His love in us. He wants to use us to love and bless others in our lives, we just need to cooperate and let Him!

A useful exercise to help us understand further what love IS is to take that scripture and turn all the characteristics into a positive form. When 1 Corinthians says, "Love is not envious," we could turn that into "Love is generous," or "Love is selfless." This just helps us to better understand what the love of God in us looks like. Fill in the chart below to continue with that process:

Love is...   # Love is not...

Patient   Impatient _____

Kind   Mean _____

Generous, Selfless _____   Envious, Jealous

_____   Boastful, Vainglorious, Haughty

_____   Conceited

_____   Selfish, Self-Seeking

_____   Rude

_____   Touchy,

_____   Fretful

_____   Resentful

_____   Takes no account of evil done by others

_____   Rejoice at Injustice

Bears up under anything   _____

Believe the bests of everyone   _____

Its hopes are fadeless   _____

Endures everything   _____

Never Fails (always wins!)   _____

The Bottom Line

What's the pay-off for the believer? Well, for one thing, the love of God never fails. As we are walking in love, we won't fulfill the desires of the flesh, so we won't be taking any of the baits either. Walking in the love of God brings such joy to the believer because it is what we are created to do. It never fails—it always wins.

The devil wants to keep us from our destiny by keeping us in strife, but he has no power to do so if we won't set our mind on the flesh. Walking in peace and love allows us to walk in God's perfect purposes in our life. We can hear God clearly when we are walking in peace and love and quickly respond to His every whisper.

So to be absolutely clear, trying to keep from taking the baits and walking in the flesh is impossible apart from walking in God's Love. We may appear righteous, but will inevitably fall at some point. The enemy is well-versed in how to trip us up. He knows our fleshly weaknesses and what to throw our way. Walking in the Love of God actually gives us margin and protection that will not only help us to avoid the baits, but also help us conform to His Word in our lives and encourage others. It also securely positions us underneath His grace and provision, which makes our peace powerful and unwavering.

The love of God was the primary motivation to solve the sin problem of the world (John 3:16). The love of God continues to be the primary motivator in solving the problems of our lives, and our eternity will be filled with enjoying the love of God for us.

Questions

1. Meditate on the scriptures found in this chapter and write down any revelations the Holy Spirit gives you.

_____

_____

_____

2. Why is it easier to stay out of strife by walking in love, instead of just trying to avoid taking the baits or control the flesh?

_____

_____

_____

Prayer of Submission to walk in Love:

Dear Father, thank You for the fruit of the Spirit that flows out of my vital relationship with You! Thank You that as I abide in You, I bear much fruit and prove to be Your disciple. Thank You that Your love has been shed abroad in my heart and that as I walk in love, I will not carry out the desires of the flesh! You are such a Good Father! You didn't want me to be in bondage to any of the baits that come along in life, so you won the victory for me through Christ and His righteousness. As I walk in the Spirit, the works of the flesh will fall away from me and I will bear the fruit of the Spirit—the fruit of love.

Scripture references:

John 15:5 — I am the vine; you are the branches. If you remain in me and I in you, you will bear much fruit; apart from me you can do nothing.

John 15:8—This is to my Father's glory, that you bear much fruit, showing yourselves to be my disciples.

Romans 5:5—And hope does not put us to shame, because God's love has been poured out into our hearts through the Holy Spirit, who has been given to us.

Romans 13:10— Love does no wrong to a neighbor; therefore love is the fulfillment of the law.

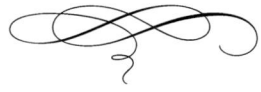

JEALOUSY

These next chapters are going to dive a little bit deeper into the root causes of many of the baits the devil uses to try and lure us out of God's Best for our lives. They are always based on lies we are tempted to believe somewhere, and if we can renew our thinking to be in line with what God says, we won't be so easily conformed to this world and its way of doing things. Many of the baits we cover in this book are birthed out of pride. We are born with infectious pride that tells us that we are just fine and everyone else is the problem. If these other people would just get their act together, our lives would be wonderful! When we become new creatures in Christ Jesus, we have to replace and reprogram our broken thinking with God's Word in order for us to be all we were created to be, and to walk in the peace we have been given.

These next 5 baits are very common in today's popular culture, and can be seen within a few moments of turning on the television. Too often we fall for what the world says is acceptable behavior and totally take ourselves right out of God's best for our lives because we don't know any differently. This is no accident! The enemy will provide as many opportunities as he can to trip us up and if we are not paying attention, we will take the bait and find ourselves out of God's peace all over again.

Jealousy

Envy, or jealousy is defined as "a feeling of discontent or covetousness with regard to another's advantages, success, possessions, etc."[2]

Being jealous opens the door for the thief to come into our lives and wreak havoc. James says,

Where do wars and fights come from among you? Do they not come from your desires for pleasure that war in your members? You lust and do not have. You murder and covet and cannot obtain. You fight and war. Yet you do not have because you do not ask. James 4:1–2a (NKJV)

For wherever there is jealousy (envy) and contention (rivalry and selfish ambition), there will also be confusion (unrest, disharmony, rebellion) and all sorts of evil and vile practices. James 3:16 (AMP)

When we allow jealousy to get a hold of us, we are telling God we aren't satisfied with what He has provided or promised. It only leads us to contention and strife. These both open the door for the thief to come in and steal from us! Don't take the bait!

Rejoice with those who rejoice, and weep with those who weep. Romans 12:15 (NASB)

If we want to maintain our peace, we can start by being thankful for what is happening in the lives of others. We don't let the enemy confuse us into thinking that if another person has something wonderful happen for them, it means that something wonderful won't happen for us. That stems from believing that there is a limited supply of God's grace. Our God is limitless! His supply is limitless! He created everything from nothing! Read these two next scriptures:

The earth is the LORD's, and everything in it, the world, and all who live in it; Psalm 24:1 (NIV)

For every animal of the forest is mine, and the cattle on a thousand hills. Psalm 50:110 (NIV)

If God owns the cattle on a thousand hills and everything in the whole world, surely He can get blessings to the other person AND US! We can know in our hearts that God is not stingy, or just into blessing everyone else. That thought comes from the enemy and is the lure to get us into jealousy. God LOVES us! Romans 8:32 states,

He who did not spare His own Son, but delivered Him over for us all, how will He not also with Him freely give us all things? (NASB)

Instead, start praising God! "God, I thank You for Your marvelous blessings in their life and I know that You have great plans for them (Jeremiah 29:11). I also thank You that You meet all my needs through Your riches in glory in Christ Jesus (Philippians 4:19)!"

When we rejoice in the blessing of others like this, we are joining in with them in glorifying what God has done! If we will rejoice over the blessings of others, we will take the power of the bait of jealousy out of our lives. We will live in peace and joy!

Once we can turn from defensive behavior into a faith-filled attitude, we can start pressing in with God for the desires of our hearts.

James tells us clearly what to do if we want something in chapter 4, verses 2b-3.

> *You do not have because you do not ask. You ask and do not receive, because you ask with wrong motives, so that you may spend it on your pleasures. (NKJV)*

God knows what we need and when we need it. It is His plan to meet our needs, on time, in full! He loves us and has good plans for us!

> *For I know the plans that I have for you,' declares the LORD, 'plans for welfare and not for calamity to give you a future and a hope. Jeremiah 29:11 (NASB)*

Jesus explained it this way in Matthew 7:11,

> *If you then, being evil, know how to give good gifts to your children, how much more will your Father who is in heaven give good things to those who ask Him! (NKJV)*

He loves us and wants us to trust in His love for us and rest in it.

> *And God is able to make all grace abound toward you, that you, always having all sufficiency in all things, may have an abundance for every good work. 2 Corinthians 9:8 (NKJV)*

In closing, as we consider that the deepest desire of the human heart is completely fulfilled in our relationship with our Father God, all these other issues are overwhelmed by the knowledge of His presence and love for us.

> *Keep your lives free from the love of money and be content with what you have, because God has said, "Never will I leave you; never will I forsake you." Hebrews 13:5 (NIV)*

When we are meditating on the fact that the Creator of the universe loves us and is always with us, we will be much more content with what we have.

Lies:

1. God blessed someone else, so there is less for me.

2. God doesn't love me as much as He loves those others.

3. I don't have enough...(money, authority, fame, time, etc.)

Truth:

1. God created everything from nothing, so getting a blessing to you is no big deal! (2 Corinthians 9:8, Matthew 7:11)

2. God didn't spare His most precious gift for you, Jesus! How will He spare anything else you might need? (Romans 8:32)

3. God will provide everything we need, when we need it, if we will just ask Him. (James 4:2a) In the meantime, we get to be content with God's wonderful presence in our lives as He will never leave us nor forsake us. (Hebrews 13:5)

Questions

1. Can you remember a time in your life when jealousy manifested in your life?

_____

_____

2. How did it negatively affect you and your relationships?

_____

_____

Prayer of Submission to avoid jealousy and to trust God:

Generous, Loving Father, I know you have only good plans for me! You meet all of my needs according to your riches in glory in Christ Jesus, and as I follow You and trust You, You will lead me into every blessing. Thank You for blessing _____ (name of someone you are struggling with jealousy against) with _____ (name of the blessing they have received from God). I know you love them as much as you love me. You are showing them Your kindness, goodness, and mercy. Help them to thoroughly enjoy Your gift of love towards them and know how much You truly love them through it. Your gifts are unlimited, and just because they have received from You doesn't diminish your plans and gifts for me too! Thank you for the gifts You have already given to me _____ (list of the blessings you have received that you are thankful to God for). Because I know You love me and Your love is in my heart, I can lean on Your love to "not be envious nor boil over with jealousy." Thank you that even more of your abounding blessings are on their way to me as well! Thank You for Your love for me, and that you have already given me your greatest blessing of Jesus! Hallelujah! Amen.

Now, pick ONE scripture from this chapter about contentment and jealousy to put on a 3x5 card in your home to meditate on and memorize. This will help you avoid the lies, walk in the spirit, and not in the flesh in this area.

UNFORGIVENESS

Unforgiveness is a major bait that the enemy effectively uses to stop the flow of the blessings of God in many people's lives. The devil has figured out that we humans want justice when others treat us unfairly, but we want mercy for ourselves. If he can't keep us from receiving mercy from God for our sins through Christ, he will try to refocus us on all those that have sinned against us. Either way, if we walk in unforgiveness, we interrupt the flow of God's grace through us to others, and everyone suffers as a result.

One of the clearest teachings on unforgiveness in the ministry of Jesus is the parable of the slave that owed his master a large sum of money found in Matthew 18:23-35.

He was unable to pay the large sum to the master, so the master had pity on him and forgave the debt instead of sending the slave and his family to prison. Immediately after this, the forgiven slave went out and found a fellow slave that owed him a small amount of money. The forgiven slave was unwilling to extend the same grace to his fellow slave, choosing to throw him into prison until every cent could be repaid. When the master of both slaves found out about this, he said to the unforgiving slave,

> *"You wicked slave, I forgave you all that debt because you pleaded with me. Should you not also have had mercy on your fellow slave, in the same way that I had mercy on you?" And his lord, moved with anger, handed him over to the torturers until he should repay all that was owed him. My heavenly Father will also do the same to you, if each of you does not forgive his brother from your heart. Matthew 18:32-35 (NKJV)*

From this parable, we can see God's perspective on when we harbor unforgiveness in our hearts against someone else. He has forgiven us of immensely more than we will ever have to forgive another person. If we doubt that, James 2:10 tells us that if we stumble over one point of the law, we have become guilty of all of it!

What do we do if someone sins against us and doesn't repent or ask for forgiveness? Or maybe they do ask, but not in the way we think they should? God tells us we need to forgive in the same way He forgave us in Christ Jesus.

> *And be kind to one another, tenderhearted, forgiving one another,*
> *even as God in Christ forgave you. Ephesians 4:32 (NKJV)*

How does God forgive us?

Does He wait until we come and plead for forgiveness for each and every sin? Does He remember our sins even after we have repented and asked for forgiveness? No! Thank You Lord!

In the story of the Prodigal Son found in Luke 15:11-32, we see this response from the father as the prodigal son returns.

> *So he got up and came to his father. But while he was still a long way*
> *off, his father saw him and felt compassion for him, and ran and*
> *embraced him and kissed him. Luke 15:20 (NASB)*

This shows the actions of a father more interested in the restoration of the relationship, than of any justice that needed to be met in order for forgiveness to be given. He had forgiven his son even before he saw his son on the road home. If one of our children had selfishly left home with their inheritance like the prodigal son did, some of us might have chosen to replay the offense over and over in our minds. We might have been tempted to "share" our rejection with our friends or family in order to feel justified in remaining in unforgiveness. Thankfully, God does not do that with us. When He says we are forgiven, we are completely and totally forgiven, and our sins and weaknesses are forgotten (Hebrews 8:12). He chose to purposefully forgive and forget our sins when He dealt with them on the cross in order to restore our fellowship with Him.

If we find ourselves struggling with unforgiveness, it may be because we haven't fully realized how much we have been forgiven. If we see our God as someone watching and waiting for us to mess up so He can punish us, we will have a hard time not doing the same thing to others. If we see our God as a judge, reminding us of our failures every time we are around Him, we will do the same to others. We have a tendency to treat others the way we think God treats us. If we struggle with unforgiveness, it could be because we haven't fully realized our forgiveness from God through Christ. Because of Jesus, God NEVER sees our sins when He looks at us. He sees His beloved son or daughter and is filled with love for us. If we struggle with criticism, we may believe that although Christ's sacrifice covered some of our sins, others still remain. Completely receiving all that Christ did for us on the cross enables us to love like He loves, to forgive like He forgives, to give like He gives.

When we come to the revelation of God's love for us, realizing that He doesn't hold any debts against us, it is SO much easier to extend grace and forgiveness to others. In Luke 7, Jesus goes to a Pharisee's home for a meal. When a "sinful" woman comes and weeps at His feet and wipes the tears with her hair, the pharisee is offended that Jesus allows such a thing. Jesus tells him a short parable to show him a facet of the character of our Heavenly Father.

> *There was a certain creditor who had two debtors. One owed five hundred denarii, and the other fifty. And when they had nothing with which to repay, he freely forgave them both. Tell Me, therefore, which of them will love him more? Luke 7:41–42 (NKJV)*

Jesus says that the creditor "freely forgave them both." He is showing us the kind of forgiveness that the Father extends to each of us. All of us were bankrupt and utterly impoverished spiritually and the Father chose to "freely forgive" us all through Jesus Christ.

> *For I will be merciful to their iniquities, and I will remember their sins no more. Hebrews 8:12 (NASB)*

He doesn't remember our sins any longer. He purposely puts them away from His mind and memory.

> *As far as the east is from the west, So far has He removed our transgressions from us. Psalms 103:12*

He thinks of us completely without reference to sin, because of what Jesus has done for us. When we come to Him for help, He doesn't consider how we snapped at our spouse 5 minutes ago, or that we were speeding on the way to church last

Sunday. He purposely removes our sins as far as the east is from the west. How then should we forgive our neighbor?

> *Bearing with one another, and forgiving each other, whoever has a complaint against anyone; just as the Lord forgave you, so also should you. Colossians 3:13 (NASB)*

This may seem like a very tall order, but evidently we can do it with His help, or He would be unjust in requiring it of us.

Remembering His great love and forgiveness for us, and all that we have needed forgiveness for is a great start.

From the beginning of my relationship with Jesus, I have always desired to serve Him by serving in church—either through playing music in praise and worship, or working in various areas where the need arose. I got saved when I was 22 and, like most new believers, was bubbling with enthusiasm. I would just jump in with most churches and start serving wherever I could.

What I discovered was that churches are more like hospitals than places where everybody has it together. In my experience, there are many people in churches who are in different places in their walks with Jesus. Some understand how to walk in love, but don't have great people skills. Some are wonderful business leaders, but are struggle to walk in love. Some are strong in their beliefs but have yet to master other areas. As a young believer, my relationships within the church walls were erratic as I worked out my salvation alongside others. There were many times that these people either hurt me with their words or actions. This really put me in the position to have to exercise forgiveness.

Over the years, Sharon and I have both had wonderful times in many different churches as we have moved across the United States. We have also had many times of pain and disappointment. God has worked in our lives and helped us to forgive other Christians for hurting us. God challenged me that whenever the devil brings the memory of the rejection or disappointment to me, I am supposed to pray for the blessings of those involved, and that they walk in the center of God's will. This is a powerful act of faith and the best thing I can do for those who hurt me. What is better than walking in the center of God's will? Plus it really burns the devil up, and I love to do that! —Greg

Lies:

1. God doesn't really expect me to forgive THEM for THAT.

2. Their sins are so much worse than mine.

3. I have a choice to forgive or not.

4. If I forgive them they will just hurt me again.

Truth:

1. Yes He does (Ephesians 4:32), and He will give you the ability and grace to do it (Philippians 2:13).

2. All sin brings death. Every sin is disobedience and separates us from God and has to be paid for—by Jesus if we will receive it, or by our eternal separation from God if we won't. There are no "little" sins to God. (Romans 3:23, 6:23)

3. Yes, you have a choice to walk in the flesh in unforgiveness, or to walk in the Spirit, and have peace, joy, and victory. That is really your only choice in regards to forgiveness. (Ephesians 4:32)

4. There is always the possibility that someone will hurt you again and again, but having God's best for your life is worth the price you pay when other repeatedly hurt you. God will repay you for your tears. (Psalm 56:8-9)

Questions

1. Who do you actively avoid in your life?

_____

_____

2. How does God want you to change in regarding these relationships?

_____

_____

Prayer of Submission to avoid unforgiveness and to trust God:

Forgiving Father, thank You for completely and fully forgiving me for all my sins—past, present, and future. There is nothing I can do that will be too big for the blood of Jesus to cleanse! There is someone that has sinned against me.

(At this point, tell God who the person is and what they did to you. It might be helpful to also tell Him how those words or actions affected you negatively. Be honest—He already knows all that is in your heart about it.)

Lord, You want me to be free from those negative affects in my life and I know that can only come as I forgive them. That doesn't mean they are free to hurt me over and over again, and I will take the proper steps to love myself and protect myself from their continued sinful behavior. But I choose to apply the forgiveness I have received in Christ to those in my life who have sinned against me too. Because You have forgiven me, I can use Your love in me to forgive them. "Love does not take into account a wrong suffered," so Your love in my heart doesn't take those sins into account as I walk in love toward them with Your strength. That doesn't mean I am unwise in trusting those that have proven themselves untrustworthy, it means I choose to be kind, patient, loving, gentle, peaceful, faithful, joyful, good, and self-controlled because that's who I am in You. Hallelujah! Amen.

Now, pick ONE scripture from this chapter about unforgiveness to put on a 3x5 card in your home to meditate on and memorize. This will help you avoid the lies, walk in the spirit, and not in the flesh in this area.

TAKING OFFENSE

[Love] does not act unbecomingly; it does not seek its own, is not provoked, does not take into account a wrong suffered,
1 Corinthians 13:5 (NASB)

Sometimes people do things that they don't apologize for, or don't consider wrong, but we can still become offended—believing they have sinned against us or hurt us in some way. This can happen when we deal with people that aren't Christians, or with Christians that aren't familiar with the Word of God, or that are just at a different place in their walk with Jesus.

Taking Offense with Other Believers

We see in 1 Corinthians 10 that Christians can have different convictions about things that are not explicitly spelled out in the Bible. Paul mentions a situation where meat that had previously been sacrificed to idols in pagan temples was being sold in the markets. He encouraged believers to...

> *Eat anything that is sold in the meat market without asking questions for conscience' sake; for the earth is the Lord's, and all it contains. If one of the unbelievers invites you and you want to go, eat anything that is set before you without asking questions for conscience' sake. But if anyone says to you, "This is meat sacrificed to idols," do not eat it, for the sake of the one who informed you, and for conscience' sake; I mean not your own conscience, but the other man's; for why is my freedom judged by another's conscience?*
> *1 Corinthians 10:25-29 (NASB)*

Some Christians could eat meat sacrificed to idols without it affecting their consciences, while others were offended by it. Paul encouraged believers to be sensitive to the consciences of others, but sometimes we don't share the areas of sensitivities in the hearts of others. It is natural for us to apply our own consciences to the lives of fellow believers, and Paul speaks against that here when he says, "why is my freedom judged by another's conscience?" That would be taking offense at the behavior or speech of someone else, and that will get us into strife and out of our love walk.

Taking Offense with Non-believers

For those around us that may not know their Savior Jesus yet, we can't really expect them to even be able to walk in the spirit and in truth. That would be like expecting a baby to be able to read and understand the dictionary. In chapter 5, we showed how our sinful flesh isn't even able to submit to God, so expecting someone without Jesus to walk in the wisdom and truth of God's Word is foolish. Our responsibility, then, to non-believers is to love them in words and actions. As we are flowing in the love of God towards them, we won't take offense because love doesn't "take into account a wrong suffered." Love forgives. Love wants what's best for others. And love never fails!

If we allow that offense to take up residence in our minds, we have forfeited our peace and freedom. It is our fleshly pride that believes we need to have an opinion about what someone else says or does. We need to forgive and release the other person(s) to God and be dedicated to walking in love with all people.

> While we were traveling over the holidays one year, we had many opportunities to become offended with each other. Six people and a carsick poodle in a minivan make for an "interesting" 800-mile trip! When situations would arise, such as having to clean up vomit off the floor mats, or trying to find a bathroom for a four year old, it would have been natural for us to become short-tempered and easily offended. But when we chose instead to walk in patience and love, and really believe that no one was "out to get us," we found even uncomfortable things pleasant, and we ended up having a lot of fun in the midst of challenges!
> —Sharon

We can't choose how people treat us, but we can choose how we respond. The enemy will try and use misunderstandings and differences of opinion to draw us into offense, which leads to argument, strife, and disunity. When we take offense at the behavior or words of someone else, we have fallen from walking in the spirit to walking in the flesh (autopilot) and the fruit of that will only produce death in some form in our relationships. It produces loss of fellowship, hurt feelings, loss of time working on things that really matter, and possibly a permanent loss of relationships. If we take the bait of offense, we will lose our peace and our effectiveness to accomplish God's will together. The situation we get into strife over is not the real issue. What's really happening is that the enemy is trying to steal God's best from us and from those around us. We don't have to let the mistakes or perceived errors of others steal our peace. If we decide in our hearts to forgive any offense—even before the offenses come—and to overlook the imperfections of others, we can live in victory in this area and walk in effective unity and powerful peace.

Lies:

1. My beliefs about an issue are the only correct beliefs.

2. I need to reveal the error of someone else's opinions.

3. I can't have fellowship with another Christian that doesn't agree with me about everything I believe is important.

Truth:

1. None of us know it all about everything. God will continue to reveal truth to us until we see Him face-to-face, and probably even after then! (1 Corinthians 13:12)

2. Being loving and understanding toward someone is more important than showing them where they are wrong. (1 Peter 4:8, 1 Corinthians 13:13)

3. If a fellow believer has an erroneous opinion about any spiritual issue, God will reveal that to them. Our job is simply to love them with the love of Christ and encourage them. (Philippians 3:15, 1 Thessalonians 5:11)

Questions

1. With whom do you have a strife-filled relationship in which you might have taken offense at something they said or did? What caused the offense? What are you going to do now?

_____

_____

_____

_____

2. Where are some other areas in your life in which you might have taken offense about something that seemed important at the time, but you now see wasn't as important as maintaining your love and peace walk?

_____

_____

_____

_____

Prayer of Submission to avoid Taking Offense and to trust God:

Patient Lord of all, Thank You for your kindness in leading me into all truth. Help me to love non-believers first and foremost. Show me where my words or actions might hinder someone from coming to You, and help me to walk in the spirit instead of the flesh in those things. Thank You that You show me the areas I need to repent and You challenge my erroneous thinking about issues that are important. I know You love me. I also believe You love my brothers and sisters in Christ and You are leading them too, so I can just relax and love them, knowing You've got this! I choose to walk in peace; I choose to walk in love! Hallelujah! Amen.

Now, pick ONE scripture from this chapter about Taking Offense to put on a 3x5 card in your home to meditate on and memorize. This will help you avoid the lies, walk in the spirit, and not in the flesh in this area.

WORRY AND SELF-CARE

So do not worry about tomorrow; for tomorrow will care for itself. Each day has enough trouble of its own. Matthew 6:34 (NASB)

Worry is a verb defined as "to torment oneself with or suffer from disturbing thoughts; fret."[3] Notice the first three words, "to torment oneself." This is the case so many times in our lives. The enemy will dangle the lure of worry or self-care in our minds when we are in a situation of which we are unsure. Worry is fear straight up, no bones about it, and <u>any decision based on fear is a bad decision</u>. Worry and self-care are our responses when negative thoughts and imaginations take up residence in our minds and hearts unchallenged. The Bible shows clearly that fear does not come from God.

For God hath not given us the spirit of fear; but of power, and of love, and of a sound mind. 2 Timothy 1:7 (KJV)

When Jesus left us His peace, He said,

"Peace I leave with you, My peace I give to you; not as the world gives do I give to you. <u>Let not your heart be troubled, neither let it be afraid</u>." John 14:27 (NASB)

Because peace is a fruit of the spirit, it will flow to us and through us as we are walking in the spirit. When we get into worry or self-care, we have traded walking in peace and the spirit for walking in the flesh.

Worry vs. Self-care

Worry is fearfully trying to figure out what to do about a problem or situation because you don't trust God to do it. It is birthed out of fear in our heart—fear that God won't do anything about it, or that God's plans aren't for our good or the good of someone else. 1 John 4:18 (AMP) states,

> *There is no fear in love [dread does not exist]. But perfect (complete, full-grown) love drives out fear, because fear involves [the expectation of divine] punishment, so the one who is afraid [of God's judgment] is not perfected in love [has not grown into a sufficient understanding of God's love].*

When we are worrying, we have forgotten how much God loves us. We have believed the lie that He won't come through for us, or that He doesn't care about us enough to do anything to help. We have forgotten that Jesus paid for all of our shortcomings, and has given us His Divine Sonship that always has God's attention and watchful care (Eph 1:5). When we remember those things, and believe they are true for us, we will act on it, and release those fears to God's Hands, knowing He will work all things out according to His wonderful plan for us. Meditating on what His plans for us are, based on His Word, will help us to recognize when our beliefs aren't right. Remember, our soul—our mind, will, emotions—has to be renewed according to the will and word of God. As we meditate on what God says about a situation, our thinking will start to fall in line with His thinking, and our fear and worry will melt away as we remember His love and faithfulness towards us in Christ.

There are two types of "self-care" in our lives today. The good type of "self-care" is a form of self-love and expresses itself by taking care of our physical bodies by eating well, exercising, brushing our teeth, and all the necessary activities to become and stay healthy. We are instructed by Paul in 1 Corinthians 6:20 to "glorify God in Your body." This isn't the form of "self-care" we are discussing in this chapter. —Sharon

A great example of this occurred to me during my college days. One morning, I noticed my car was sitting on empty and I had a 20 minute drive to get to school. I knew that if some way I was able to make it to class, there was no way I would be able to get back home without gas in my tank—and money to pay for it! I couldn't actually do anything about it at that time, so I just prayed a prayer that went something like this, "Lord, you know I need gas to get home tonight. I'm letting you figure this out because I've got nothing." Then I just totally forgot about it. I honestly didn't give it another thought the rest of the morning and early afternoon until a friend of mine came by and wanted to pay me for typing up his paper for him a week or so before. I had done it as a favor to him, but he insisted that God wanted him to pay me $10 for it. I tried to refuse the money, (because I had honestly forgotten I needed it!) but he persisted and I took the cash. As I was leaving work that late afternoon, I realized what God had done. As I had rested and chosen not to worry about the situation I couldn't control, He had worked on my behalf. —Sharon

God is working all around us, all the time, and wants to work on our behalf, but we have to get out of His way and let Him. He's not just going to take over without your permission. If you want to try and figure out the situation, rather than trust in His wisdom and love for you, He will let you try. Self-care, as a bait, is our attempt to depend on our OWN strength, our OWN logic and problem-solving skills, or our OWN abilities to solve a problem. It is birthed out of our pride that tells us, "I've got this! I don't need any help from God." Paul addresses this tendency of our flesh in Philippians 3:3 (AMP),

> ...for we [who are born-again have been reborn from above—
> spiritually transformed, renewed, set apart for His purpose and]
> are the true circumcision, who worship in the Spirit of God and
> glory and take pride and exult in Christ Jesus and place no confidence
> [in what we have or who we are] in the flesh—

God wants us to think well of ourselves, to believe in the gifts and abilities He has given to us, but He doesn't want us to believe that we can do anything apart from Him in our lives and hearts. Remember what Jesus tells us in John 15:5 as He is encouraging the disciples to abide in Him, saying, "I am the vine, you are the branches; he who abides in Me and I in him, he bears much fruit, for apart from Me you can do nothing." When we are relying on ourselves to figure things out, or fix things, we are cutting ourselves off from the flow of what God is doing in our lives. When we insist on doing things without His help, we will fall far short of the good things He wants for us. Instead, if we choose to tell Him, "I can do nothing without You. Please show me how to handle this situation. You are wiser than I am, and I can't do this without You," we are humbling ourselves and submitting to God and His way of doing things. We will find His grace to triumph in every situation because

> *...He gives a greater grace. Therefore it says, "God is opposed to the proud, but gives grace to the humble." Submit therefore to God. Resist the devil and he will flee from you. Draw near to God and He will draw near to you. James 4:6-8 (NASB)*

and

> *"Humble yourselves in the presence of the Lord, and He will exalt you" James 4:10 (NASB)*

I got saved by accepting Jesus as my Lord and Savior at the age of 22. Sharon and I met just a few weeks after my conversion and were married a year later. Married life was certainly an adventure and there were lots of opportunities for me to provide leadership for our young family. I was clueless in so many ways and usually fell back on just using my intellect and intuition rather than going to God in prayer and waiting on His instruction. Most men are trained by society to just "slay the dragon" by whatever means necessary, and the hard part is that they seem to get a certain amount of success in doing so. This reinforces in them that they did the "right" thing since the problem is gone. This type of decision making is "self-care" and not what God wants for us. God has an opinion and wants to share it with you, giving you guidance and wisdom beyond your years. Self-care, meaning doing it my way apart from His wisdom, cost me and my family in more ways than I care to remember. Glory to God that He was patient with me, and taught me how to seek His face in prayer and not lean on my own abilities to lead our family and solve problems. His ways are far above my ways, His thoughts above my thoughts (Isaiah 55:9), and I am forever grateful for His grace. He has been so faithful to help me grow in leading our family —Greg

1. Which of these two baits, worry or self-care, do you tend to struggle with the most? What lies are you believing that leads to that bait in your life?

_____

_____

_____

_____

_____

Worry and Self-care Affect Our Health

Our bodies were not designed to bear the weight of worries and cares for long periods of time. Consistently choosing to keep these things in our hearts instead of casting them on our Father will affect our peace and health.

> _"For this reason I say to you, do not be worried about your life,_
> _as to what you will eat or what you will drink; nor for your body,_
> _as to what you will put on. Is not life more than food, and the body_
> _more than clothing? Look at the birds of the air, that they do not sow,_
> _nor reap nor gather into barns, and yet your heavenly Father feeds_
> _them. Are you not worth much more than they? And who of you by_
> _being worried can add a single hour to his life?_
> _Matthew 6:25-27 (NASB)_

Jesus is showing us here that worry doesn't help even a little bit. It can't add any time to our life span; it doesn't do anything positive for us, but cuts us off from the flow of walking in the spirit. In Mark 4, Jesus tells us that worry stops the work of God's word in our hearts to produce the good fruit we need.

> _...but the worries of the world, and the deceitfulness of riches, and the_
> _desires for other things enter in and choke the word, and it becomes_
> _unfruitful. Mark 4:19 (NASB)_

God wants us to cast all these situations on His very capable lap. He loves us. He wants to help us. Our fear keeps us from trusting Him to help us. Our pride keeps us from letting Him help us. He isn't overbearing or bossy. He won't interject Himself into our situations without our permission. He wants us to freely choose to let Him help us because we see our desperate need and His wonderful love and care for us. Every test, trial, or tribulation is an opportunity for us to get to know Him better, to see His faithfulness to us as we rest in His love for us and His amazing power to do what we cannot.

> *Therefore humble yourselves under the mighty hand of God, that He may exalt you at the proper time, casting all your anxiety on Him, because He cares for you. 1 Peter 5:6-7 (NASB)*

He wants to help us with every problem. He actively sought us out when we were far from Him in our sinful states, and He hasn't changed His mind about wanting to help us with everything else in our lives. When we believe this, we will walk in peace and trust that no matter what the problem is, He has the answer.

> *What then shall we say to these things? If God is for us, who is against us? He who did not spare His own Son, but delivered Him over for us all, how will He not also with Him freely give us all things? Romans 8:31-32 (NASB)*

2. Has worry or self-care affected your health in any way? How?

_____

_____

_____

_____

_____

Trusting God Is Our New Normal

In our spirit, we trust God, leading us to make the wise decisions that lead us to life and peace. In our flesh, we fret, worry, and self-care, making foolish and rushed decisions that lead us to death in our relationships or even our health. We can't let fear be the reason we do or don't do things. As soon as we realize we are making a decision based on fear, we need to back up and get our head on straight. **Remember, any decision based on fear is a bad decision.**

> *Do not fret; **it leads only to evildoing.** Psalm 37:8b (NASB)*

Replaying a situation over and over in our minds is one way we know we are worrying. If there is something we know God wants us to do about a situation, we need to joyfully obey, knowing His will for us is only going to bring us good things. If there really is nothing we can do about it, we need to let it go to God. When we hold on to these distressing imaginations and worries, we are tormenting our hearts. This is the "torment" that John talks about in 1 John 4:18. It only serves to paralyze us into inaction or drives us to perform the wrong action.

Fear Lies

Fear is one of the enemy's greatest and most effective weapons against us. Who hasn't been afraid of something at one point in their lives? When we were kids, we were afraid of what was under the bed or in the closet. As we grew up, our fears morphed into something more "realistic" based on the experiences of others we know or what we read about in the news. But those things we fear don't actually exist in the present. And when we are focused on preventing some negative thing we don't want to happen, we **aren't** meditating on who and what we are in Christ, and Who and W hat He is to us. God loves us and only wants good things for us!

> For I know the plans and thoughts that I have for you,' says the Lord, 'plans for peace and well-being and not for disaster, to give you a future and a hope. Jeremiah 29:11 (AMP)

> Every good thing given and every perfect gift is from above, coming down from the Father of lights, with whom there is no variation or shifting shadow. James 1:17 (NASB)

Fear will come. It is a spirit sent from the devil to derail our trust in God and His good will for us. The point here isn't whether or not fear will come and try to influence us, but rather WHEN it does, what do we do?

> Be anxious for nothing, but in everything by prayer and supplication with thanksgiving let your requests be made known to God. Philippians 4:6 (NASB)

First, we can answer fear with prayer and trust in God. We share the negative thoughts we are battling with the Lord, ask for His supply that meets every need, and thank Him for what we have been given in Christ. God has already answered all of these fearful imaginations with the promises in His Word. If we don't know what He has given us, we just need to read His Word and find out! (A concordance of the Bible or google search for scriptures about the topic you are struggling with is a great way to find out what His Word says about anything!) Fear is not from God and He doesn't want us to be afraid. He wants us to live in peace and hope as we trust in Him!

> *May the God of hope fill you with all joy and peace as you trust in him, so that you may overflow with hope by the power of the Holy Spirit. Romans 15:13 (NIV)*

Lies:

1. If I don't do something about this situation, nothing or something bad will happen.

2. God doesn't want to help me with this.

3. God can't help me with this.

Truth:

1. If we don't let God do something about the situation, nothing will happen. (Matthew 19:26)

2. "He who did not spare His own Son, but delivered Him over for us all, how will He not also with Him freely give us all things?" (Romans 8:32 ,NASB)

3. There is NOTHING too difficult for God. (Jeremiah 32:27)

Prayer of Submission to avoid Worry and Self-care and to trust God:

Glorious and Powerful Father, thank You for loving me so much. You didn't spare Your only Son, but delivered Him up for me. I'm in awe! But honestly Lord, I'm still struggling with _____ (list your concerns here). You have already given me everything I need for life and Godliness in Christ Jesus! I have no reason or need to worry or to try and solve my problems all by myself. You love me and have only good plans for me. I am filled with all joy and peace as I trust in You, and my hope overflows by the power of the Holy Spirit! I will not fear but be filled with power, love, and a sound mind! Hallelujah! Amen.

Now, pick ONE scripture from this chapter about Worry and Self-care to put on a 3x5 card in your home to meditate on and memorize. This will help you avoid the lies and walk in the spirit, not in the flesh, in this area.

3. What scriptures can help you renew your mind so that you don't give in to worry or self-care in the future?

_____

_____

_____

CRITICISM

Love does not dishonor others, it is not self-seeking, it is not easily angered, it keeps no record of wrongs. (NIV)

We all know what it means to be critical of someone else. Finding fault with others is as old as time. Going all the way back to the garden of Eden, we see Adam blaming God for giving him Eve in an attempt to deflect his guilt in having eaten the forbidden fruit (Genesis 3:12). Being critical of others is a work of the flesh and opens us to strife.

Criticism occurs when our focus is on our own "rightness," and the "wrongness" of others. It is birthed out of pride in our hearts, and rises up in us when our focus has strayed from Jesus and His perfection to our own self-perceived good qualities. It begins with prideful and critical thoughts, and proceeds to critical and caustic words pretty quickly if left unchallenged by our spirits.

Are you saying I can't be critical of anyone?

No, we can be critical all day long if we want to, but we need to be prepared to not walk in the spirit and powerful peace if we choose to do that.

Let's look at 1 Corinthians 13:5:

Love does not dishonor others, it is not self-seeking, it is not easily angered, it keeps no record of wrongs. (NIV)

This section of scripture is defining "Love"—more specifically, "God's Love"—and what love does and doesn't do. We can see that God's love in us doesn't dishonor others, and doesn't keep a record of what they do wrong. These two things alone make a good case against criticism.

What if someone is criticizing me?

This is a tough situation, especially if the criticism is coming from someone we care about. That can make it especially painful to deal with. Let's look at what Jesus did under those same circumstances.

> *When they hurled their insults at him, he did not retaliate; when he suffered, he made no threats. Instead, he entrusted himself to him who judges justly. 1 Peter 2:23 (NIV)*

By the power of the Holy Spirit, Jesus trusted in His Father. Because He left us His peace, we can trust God too! We can remember that His opinion about us is the only one that really matters, and He loves and accepts us utterly and completely!

Now, what about correction?

> *Let no unwholesome word proceed from your mouth, but only such a word as is good for edification according to the need of the moment, so that it will give grace to those who hear. Ephesians 4:29 (NASB)*

It is generally best not to have an opinion about anyone else or their behavior, but there are a few instances where this is permitted and actually beneficial. God gives us permission to correct those directly under our authority, such as our children or subordinates in an organization. This should only be done for their edification. God gives us the grace to encourage and discipline those under our authority, without getting out of His peace, if we will do it in love. Even Jesus abided by this principle in Luke 12 when a man asked Him to intervene in a personal family dispute.

> *Someone in the crowd said to Him, "Teacher, tell my brother to divide the family inheritance with me." But He said to him, "Man, who appointed Me a judge or arbitrator over you?" Luke 12:13-14 (NASB)*

As the Son of God, Jesus had every right to dictate what any person should or shouldn't do, but as a human being, a "Son of Man," He didn't have direct authority over this man's brother and responded in that way. Jesus went on to challenge this man's heart with a parable about greed and challenged him to be rich toward God, not the world. The only brother Jesus had earthly authority over in this scenario was the one that came to Him, and submitted to Him as his "Teacher." Jesus answered him accordingly, without even addressing whether the inheritance should be shared, in principle, or not.

What about "constructive criticism?"

Pride deceives us (Obadiah 1:3) into thinking we are helping when we aren't. In Matthew 7:3-5, Jesus illustrates what can happen when we criticize.

Why do you look at the speck that is in your brother's eye, but do not notice the log that is in your own eye? Or how can you say to your brother, 'Let me take the speck out of your eye,' and behold, the log is in your own eye? You hypocrite, first take the log out of your own eye, and then you will see clearly to take the speck out of your brother's eye. (NASB)

This "log" can be pride in our hearts. The "speck" can be a lie someone is believing. We can't clearly take the lie out with the washing of the water of the Word (Ephesians 5:26), if we are swinging the pride log around and whacking people in the head! If we REALLY want to help people, we need to let the Holy Spirit take the log out of our own eyes, whatever it may be, and then we can see clearly to help others.

I remember when we brought our firstborn son home from the hospital. I had no real experience with babies, so I was very nervous and unsure about how to do just about everything! My husband has two siblings that are quite a bit younger than he is, so he had a pretty good idea what to do most of the time. After a few months of staying at home full time with my son, I had picked up a few skills and had become pretty proficient at the whole mothering thing. I started to notice that my husband wasn't holding our son right. He failed to get the water temperature just right for his baths, and didn't get him as clean as I could. He didn't even realize he was putting on diapers the wrong way! I started voicing these tips and it started causing some problems in our peace levels for some reason—weird, right? I clearly remember the Lord speaking gently to my heart that I had learned these skills through trial and error in my parenting, and I needed to give my husband the freedom and patience to do the same thing.
—Sharon

It's not going to hurt anyone if our spouse puts the diaper on the wrong way, or uses too much soap to wash our son's hair. We need to lighten up on so many of the things we let upset us throughout the day. There are so few things that are truly important—really only OneJesus! When we aren't in authority over someone else, there is no reason for us to have an opinion about how they wear their ties, or how much perfume they put on. God made us all different ON PURPOSE, so everyone else is going to think differently, speak differently, and behave differently than we would. That's ok! God still loves them as much as He loves us! And because of His love in us, we can love them too! And as we let go of the critical attitude, we will see the blessing that God has placed in that other person for us. God made us all different on purpose, especially in the body of Christ, and we need each other's differences to fulfill God's purposes here on the earth.

Some examples of criticism:

- Not agreeing with how our spouse is doing the dishes, making the bed, changing a diaper, etc.
- Having a negative opinion of other drivers on the way to work in the morning.
- Thinking we could do a better job than someone else waiting our table, or serving us in a fast food line.
- Holding the idea that a neighbor or relative should take better care of their lawn, their children, their cars, etc.
- Practicing conversations in our head with people for when we see them next. This is the classic "Just wait till the next time I see this person, I'm going to give them a piece of my mind." Practicing arguments or heated discussion is practicing sin.

How should we respond to the sin of others?

When we see someone struggling with walking in the flesh, whether they are a fellow believer or not, we will have compassion and mercy if we are responding in the spirit and walking in love. If our first response is to criticize them in our hearts, then we too, are operating out of the flesh and we are going to stumble. Our critical attitude needs to be a "red flag" to us, signaling that we need to spend time with Jesus to set our minds again on the spirit. We have a great example of walking in the spirit in this regard in the book of Jude, verses 20-23.

But you, beloved, building yourselves up on your most
holy faith, praying in the Holy Spirit, keep yourselves in the love
of God, waiting anxiously for the mercy of our Lord Jesus Christ
to eternal life. And have mercy on some, who are doubting; save
others, snatching them out of the fire; and on some have mercy with
fear, hating even the garment polluted by the flesh. (NASB)

Jude commends us to keep ourselves—literally to guard ourselves—in God's love for us. When we are walking in the spirit and love, we respond out of mercy on those who are struggling, endeavor to rescue others from destruction, and on some show mercy with caution, so we don't get drawn into the same sin or strifeful criticism and judgment of it and end up in bondage also. As we continue to read in Jude, we see who actually keeps us from messing up in our lives.

Now to Him who is able to keep you from stumbling, and to make you
stand in the presence of His glory blameless with great joy,
to the only God our Savior, through Jesus Christ our Lord, be glory,
majesty, dominion and authority, before all time and now and forever.
Amen. Jude 24-25 (NASB)

As we continue to abide in Him and in His love for us, we are kept safe from stumbling with criticism or with any of the other baits that would come to trip us up. And because it is all through Him, He is glorified in us.

Lies:

1. They are doing it wrong and I need to tell them.

2. They will thank me in the future for all my wise advice and correction.

3. They would want me to say something to them if they knew how wrong they are.

4. If they don't change, my life will be negatively affected.

5. It would be mean to let them keep doing it the wrong way.

Truth:

1. God's love in us doesn't pay attention to the wrong it sees in others, or feel the need to proudly display itself. (1 Corinthians 13:4-5)

2. What somebody else does is none of our concern. (Proverbs 26:17)

3. God's love in us doesn't draw attention to itself or "display itself haughtily." (1 Corinthians 13:4)

4. God is working all things out for you according to the kind intention of His will. He will work any situation out for your best, if you let Him. Just trust Him and walk the spirit. (Romans 8:28, Ephesians 1:5, Hebrews 1:13)

5. They belong to God and He will deal with them at the right time, in the right way. (Romans 14:4)

Questions

1. How have you been critical of others this past week?

_____

_____

_____

_____

_____

_____

_____

2. Why is walking in the spirit and love such a great defense against being critical of others?

_____

_____

_____

_____

_____

_____

Prayer of Submission to avoid Criticism and to trust God:

Merciful and Patient Lord, Thank You for dealing with me as with a son/daughter, which is what You have made me to be. I can see now that my pride has deceived me into being critical of others in the past, and I repent of it. Only You can truly see the state of others and their spiritual and emotional needs, and even what causes them to do what they do. Only You can truly change us from the inside out, and I repent for trying to change others according to my idea of what they "should" be. Please help me to see others through Your Spirit and Your love. Help me to see and rejoice in the gifts You have placed within them. And help me to only encourage them as they grow in their walk with You. If they don't have a walk with You yet, help me to respond in mercy because I have received so much mercy from You in so many ways. Let me be led by Your Holy Spirit in all these things as I guard myself in Your love for me. Thank You! Hallelujah! Amen.

Now, pick ONE scripture from this chapter about Criticism to put on a 3x5 card in your home to meditate on and memorize. This will help you avoid the lies and walk in the spirit, not in the flesh, in this area.

JUDGMENT

Do not judge so that you will not be judged. For in the way you judge, you will be judged; and by your standard of measure, it will be measured to you. Matthew 7:1-2 (NASB)

The root of the word judgment is the word "judge." What do judges do? They sit and listen to the accusations about the defendants, examine evidence that supports or refutes the accusations, and then pronounce a verdict and, if a guilty verdict is reached, condemn defendants to a form of punishment. Judges play a crucial role in our legal system, and we are very thankful for their service in the administration of justice. However, when it comes to you and me, Jesus has a different idea about whether judgment is acceptable in our lives. In Matthew 7:1, Jesus says:

Judge not, that you be not judged. Matthew 7:1 (NKJV)

Jesus is describing the judgments we can make against other people. If we keep reading, Jesus tells us why we shouldn't judge others.

For with what judgment you judge, you will be judged; and with the measure you use, it will be measured back to you. Matthew 7:2 (NKJV)

When we choose to act according to the flesh and judge someone else, we place ourselves in God's place as Judge of humanity. Jesus was trying to warn us much like a parent warns their children not to touch a hot pot on the stove or play with matches. The crop we will reap from sowing seeds of judgment, is more judgment upon our own heads! So if we are to heed God's warning to not judge others, we then need to know exactly what judgment is so we can avoid it.

Judgment has 3 parts to it:

1. Judging people's motives—specifically, **believing we know why they do what they do.**

2. Judging people's thoughts or **believing we know what someone is thinking.**

3. **Condemning people's actions** (having a negative opinion).

These are the primary facets that make up judgment. Let's look at these more closely.

Parts 1 & 2 - Judging Motives and Knowing the Thoughts of Others

We have combined these into one because they are closely related. Let's ask ourselves a simple question.

Can we read the mind of another person?

The answer is no, we cannot. The action of judging others' thoughts and motives is something we technically are unable to do. Paul wrote:

> *For what man knows the things of a man except the spirit of the man which is in him? Even so no one knows the things of God except the Spirit of God. 1 Corinthians 2:11 (NKJV)*

When we think about it, it's kind of silly to believe we can do this, but people do this to each other every day. Someone will be in an argument and say "You did this because...." or "I know that you are thinking..." and use it as a basis to try and beat the other person in an argument or have an excuse to be critical. All it does is allow strife to enter into the situation and interrupt God's peace. It's not worth the trade. Don't take the bait!

Part 3 - Condemning people's actions.

Condemn is defined as "to express an unfavorable or adverse judgment on; indicate strong disapproval of; to pronounce to be guilty; sentence to punishment."4 In other words, to have a negative opinion about other people and their actions, and to believe they are worthy of punishment accordingly. It is amazing how pervasive this is in our popular culture, especially on television and social media. This is a crafty bait that hurts believers and their relationships everyday. Let's look at how Jesus handled this bait when He was put in this type of situation.

And the scribes and Pharisees brought unto him a woman taken in adultery; and when they had set her in the midst, They say unto him, "Master, this woman was taken in adultery, in the very act. Now Moses in the law commanded us, that such should be stoned: but what sayest thou?" This they said, tempting him, that they might have to accuse him. But Jesus stooped down, and with his finger wrote on the ground, as though he heard them not. So when they continued asking him, he lifted up himself, and said unto them, "He that is without sin among you, let him first cast a stone at her." And again he stooped down, and wrote on the ground. And they which heard it, being convicted by their own conscience, went out one by one, beginning at the eldest, even unto the last: and Jesus was left alone, and the woman standing in the midst. When Jesus had lifted up himself, and saw none but the woman, he said unto her, "Woman, where are those thine accusers? Hath no man condemned thee?" She said, "No man, Lord." And Jesus said unto her, "Neither do I condemn thee: go, and sin no more." John 8:3-11 (KJV)

This woman was surrounded by religious leaders that were condemning her and her behavior. They were legally correct that she deserved to be stoned according to Mosaic law. Jesus didn't disagree with this, He merely pointed out that the condemners were also worthy of condemnation. The only person in that crowd that was righteous enough to condemn her to death was Jesus Himself, because He knew no sin (1 Corinthians 5:21). But He didn't condemn her either, and charged her to "go and sin no more." The world would have us believe that the right thing to do is to judge and condemn others when they make a mistake. However, when we realize that we are all guilty and worthy of the punishment of death for our own sins, the desire to condemn someone else for their sins seems to fall away. Just in case we are still wondering how God feels about condemnation, we can read this:

For God did not send his Son into the world to condemn the world, but to save the world through him. John 3:17 (NIV)

Notice that this is the next verse right after the most famous scripture of all, John 3:16.

For God so loved the world, that He gave His only begotten Son, that whoever believes in Him shall not perish, but have eternal life. (NIV)

God is more interested in building up relationships than tearing them down with judgment. He also seems to indicate that condemning the world does not accomplish salvation for the world. If we want to walk in powerful peace and be an instrument of God in the lives of others, we need to stay away from having an opinion about someone else's behavior, especially if we actually want to be influential in their lives. Honestly, we have enough to do just keeping ourselves out of trouble!

> *Who are you to judge the servant of another? To his own master he stands or falls; and he will stand, for the Lord is able to make him stand. Romans 14:4 (NASB)*

We can remember this when we are tempted, and it will defuse the enemy's attempts to lure us away from walking in peace.

A great example of the principle of not having an opinion about things that do not concern us is when we give gifts to other people. Sometimes when we give things to others, they do not treat the gifts with the same care as we did or would like them to. Choosing to have an opinion about how they care for the gifts is a trap laid by the enemy! If we give something to someone, it is no longer ours—it is theirs to do with as they want. This means we should not allow ourselves to have an opinion about them regarding how they treat those gifts. This is strictly between them and the Lord, and does not concern us in the least. Having an opinion about it will steal our peace! Understanding this and being mindful of it will keep us from being critical and getting into strife. This will be tough at first, but keeping our eyes on God's best for OUR lives will make it much easier to ignore the traps set for us.

> *There is therefore now no condemnation to them which are in Christ Jesus, who walk not after the flesh, but after the Spirit. Romans 8:1 (KJV)*

Criticism, judgment, and condemnation are not acceptable tools and do not belong in the tool belt of the believer! Using these does not produce righteousness and give grace into the lives of others. Instead, these tools will produce offense, strife, anger, and disharmony in our lives and the lives of those around us.

1. Who in your life have you judged this week? How did you judge that person?

_____

_____

_____

_____

_____

_____

_____

_____

Why do we judge others?

Judging the thoughts and motives of others or condemning their behavior can all be rooted in pride. We can believe we have some "secret knowledge" about someone else that disparages their character, or makes us feel better about who we are and what we have done. We begin to believe we are "better" than they are somehow, or more mature in our Christian walk than they are. When we do this, we are putting ourselves in the place of God and His Word as the ultimate authority on right and wrong. James speaks of this in James 4:11-12,

> _Do not speak against one another, brethren. He who speaks against a brother or judges his brother, speaks against the law and judges the law; but if you judge the law, you are not a doer of the law but a judge of it. There is only one Lawgiver and Judge, the One who is able to save and to destroy; but who are you who judge your neighbor?(NASB)_

James shows us clearly here that our job isn't to make sure others are obeying God's law, but to let the Lord be the Lawgiver and Judge of others. He knows what's really going on in their hearts and He can do the right thing, at the right time, and in the right way to help them grow in Him.

2. Look back at your example of judgment in the previous question. Was this judgment based on pride in your heart? (If you didn't fill that section out, please do it now. God wants you to be free to walk in love and peace, but we have to be honest with Him and submit to Him first.)

_____

_____

_____

_____

_____

_____

_____

_____

_____

Another reason we judge the thoughts and motives or condemn the actions of others can be rooted in fear. When we have been hurt in some way, emotionally or physically, we begin telling ourselves stories about _why_ that happened so that we can avoid it in the future. This is a defense mechanism we use to try and keep us from being hurt in a similar situation in the future, but it can thwart our ability to have meaningful, healthy relationships. As we start to believe these stories about _why_ others have hurt us in the past, it can affect how we view the actions of everyone else, even if they aren't involved in the painful situation. We try to interpret the meanings behind the words and actions of others so we can avoid people we believe will hurt us in the same way we were hurt before. This can lead to miscommunication and misinterpretation and produce strife in our relationships. We have to trust the Lord to keep us safe and keep us away from dangerous people. Staying in forgiveness is a great way to be able to see clearly in this regard. As our hearts are clean, we can clearly hear the Holy Spirit's wisdom regarding our relationships and walk right where He wants us to walk—in love and peace and safety!

3. Was your example of judgment listed earlier based on fear in your heart? (If you didn't fill that section out, please do it now. God wants you to be free to walk in love and peace, but we have to be honest with Him and submit this situation to Him first.)

_____

_____

_____

_____

_____

_____

Judgment based on pride or fear is from our unrenewed mind on the flesh and can only produce death in our lives. God wants us to walk in love with a mind set on the spirit, which only produces life and peace! As we walk in the spirit in this way, there is a place for a type of judgment rooted in the love of God for us and others.

Spiritual Discernment

There is a place for judgment within the body of Christ mentioned by Paul in 1 Corinthians 5. Verse 1 starts this teaching with a review of the facts of a serious situation.

> _It is actually reported that there is immorality among you, and immorality of such a kind as does not exist even among the Gentiles, that someone has his father's wife._
> _1 Corinthians 5:1 (NASB)_

It had been reported to Paul that a man within the Corinthian church was living with his step-mother as his wife. It sounds like this degree of immorality was even unheard of among the heathen in Corinth, so it was exceedingly grievous for Paul (and for God) that it was found within the church. Evidently, word of this situation had gotten out and was giving the Corinthian church a bad reputation among the lost they were trying to win for Christ. Paul rebukes the church for not confronting this immorality and putting away this sin, or this sinner if he chose not to repent. The Corinthians would have preserved the good Name of Jesus and their reputation as God's people if they had instead judged this immorality and removed it from their midst.

This form of judgment is also translated as "determination," as in to determine between a good or evil, or to discern. We are encouraged many times in scripture to discern good behavior and fruit from bad behavior and fruit and to act accordingly. In this sense, believers are admonished to judge or discern behavior and avoid those people that exhibit evil behavior and fruit and are unrepentant about it.

In one of the final chapters of 1 Corinthians, Paul goes on to explain why we need to appear different from the lost in the world as he says,

> Do not be deceived: "Bad company corrupts good morals." Become sober-minded as you ought, and stop sinning; for some have no knowledge of God. I speak this to your shame. 1 Corinthians 15:33-34 (NASB)

He is sharing the wise principle that we will look like those we keep company with. If we begin to look like the world, and engage in the same sins they are, we can't reflect the image of God to the lost in our midst. Paul was disappointed in the Corinthians because those needing salvation weren't able to get to know God by getting to know the Corinthian believers.

Our responsibility as believers is to accurately reflect the goodness and glory of God to the lost world around us, and walking in this form of judgment, or discernment, is part of that. However, this doesn't include judging the thoughts or motives of another, or condemning someone for the sins they engage in. There is no way for us to know what is in the mind or heart of another in the natural, so we need to stay away from those things that will cause us to walk in fleshly pride or fear. Paul shows this distinction clearly in 1 Corinthians 11:31 when he says,

> But if we judged ourselves rightly, we would not be judged. But when we are judged, we are disciplined by the Lord so that we will not be condemned along with the world. (NASB)

As we choose to abide in Him, our focus will naturally be on Jesus and not on ourselves or others. Our spirits, vitally connected to Jesus, will automatically discern evil and be drawn to what is good. We won't even consider judging our neighbor because we are walking in love, and love believes the best of others. Let's be honest, we really can't keep people from being hurtful to us. We simply don't have the ability to know who, what, where, or how the threats to our lives will come. Only God can truly protect us in every way. The good news is that He loves us so deeply and we can trust Him to protect us from all evil.

Lies:

1. I can figure out why someone does what they do, and I should.

2. I have the right to condemn the sin I see in others.

3. Knowing what someone else is thinking is going to protect me.

Truth:

1. In the natural, there is no way we can know what is in someone else's heart. (1 Corinthians 2:11)

2. If God didn't send Jesus into the world to condemn it, He didn't send you into the world to condemn it either. Condemnation doesn't help anyone. (John 3:17)

3. Our job is to love others and trust God. He is our protector and our guard. (Psalm 127:1)

Prayer of Submission to avoid Judgment and to trust God:

Omniscient and Omnipotent Father God, You alone know all things and yet You love and accept me utterly and completely because of Christ! It was even Your idea to send Him to redeem me! Thank You! Because You love and care for me so much, I can trust you to protect me from harm. I can trust You to show me who I need to stay away from and keep me from the evil one. I choose to follow Your Holy Spirit in all things and let You lead me in my relationships, trusting You to keep me safe and use me to lead others to You. I repent of trying to figure out why people do what they do, only You can truly know that. I repent of trying to figure out what people are thinking, only You can truly know that as well. I repent of condemning the sin I see in others, either in my mind and heart, or verbally. You didn't send Jesus to condemn sin in the world, in fact you sent Him to take all of our condemnation on Himself, so I have no good reason to condemn anyone. Thank You for helping me to see the truth, and for the strength and desire to walk in it! Hallelujah! Amen.

Now, pick ONE scripture from this chapter about Judgment to put on a 3x5 card in your home to meditate on and memorize. This will help you avoid the lies and walk in the spirit, not in the flesh, in this area.

GOSSIP, SLANDER & TALEBEARING

He who goes about as a slanderer reveals secrets, therefore do not associate with a gossip. Proverbs 20:19 (NASB)

Our flesh can try to insert itself in so many places in our lives, and it can be hard for us to see it when everyone else around us is engaging in the same fleshly, carnal behavior. One such area occurs in our manner of speech.

Gossip and Slander

Gossip is defined as "idle talk or rumor, especially about the personal or private affairs of others."[5] Another description is to discuss something about another person that defames their character. Paul speaks about young widows not to be given financial help from the church because,

> *At the same time they also learn to be idle, as they go around from house to house; and not merely idle, but also gossips and busybodies, talking about things not proper to mention. 1 Timothy 5:13 (NASB)*

We all know that gossip is "bad," but so many people participate in gossip even though they know it is unacceptable. The unfortunate thing about gossip is that it not only hurts the person's reputation who is being discussed, it also hurts the person(s) who are participating in it.

Here's how this works. Jane is talking to her good friend Lynn, saying "Did you hear about Susie? She is pregnant. And she is not married!" Jane has not only traded her peace to gossip about Susie, but she has damaged Susie's reputation to Lynn so that the next time Lynn sees Susie, she will remember what was said about her.

We have come up with an effective visual to help better illustrate this action, and it is one most of us are familiar with: vomit. Jane has basically vomited this gossip into Lynn's head and now Lynn has to walk around with it in her thought-life. It may seem a little graphic, but we need to take gossip as seriously as God does.

What do we do if we have heard a juicy tidbit of gossip?

If we are walking in the spirit, and walking in love, we won't engage in gossip because love works no ill to a neighbor and love fulfills the intention of the law. Our hearts are moved by God's love to believe only the best of others and to have mercy on them where they struggle, knowing that we struggle sometimes in our lives as well. Love will try and protect the reputation of someone else and keeps confidences. We can't do any of these things when we are in the flesh, but through Christ we can do all these things!

Why is gossip a temptation for us?

There is a part of us that wants to be noticed, accepted, and celebrated. Sometimes we give in to insecurities and the need to feel important, and think distributing the latest gossip will help with that. This reveals our mind set on the the flesh and feeds our pride. When we seek and obtain our sense of worth from who God says we are, and how important He thinks we are, we are much less likely to fall for this particular bait because our mind will be set on the spirit instead. When we are secure in knowing we are loved, it matters little to us what a neighbor might think, and we won't harm the reputations of others by gossiping about them.

> *We love, because He first loved us. If someone says, "I love God," and hates his brother, he is a liar; for the one who does not love his brother whom he has seen, cannot love God whom he has not seen. And this commandment we have from Him, that the one who loves God should love his brother also. 1 John 4:19-21 (NASB)*

How do we stop others from gossiping in our presence?

One way is to change the direction of the conversation. People love to talk about themselves, and an off-the-cuff question about them, even unrelated to the gossipy conversation, can completely steer discussion to a more positive avenue. An example of this would be to ask if that person has any vacation plans coming up soon, or a concert they are planning to go to, or if there is anything they are looking forward to. If there is nothing we can do to stop the gossip from occurring, we may need to leave the situation entirely. We can excuse ourselves to the restroom, or choose to simply walk away if that wouldn't be rude.

He who goes about as a slanderer reveals secrets, therefore do not associate with a gossip. Proverbs 20:19 (NASB)

What's amazing is that when our attitude is to walk in love with others, it may actually change their behavior and attitudes. When people feel truly loved and accepted, they don't feel the need to prove their worth by belittling others. When we let the love of God touch the lives of others through us, they are changed in His presence. All of a sudden, instead of strife and discord, we are sowing peace into the lives of others. We are peacemakers! As we pray for others and walk in peace and love, the gossipers will be put to shame, not us! So when someone starts to tell us a bit of gossip, we can either step in there, and gently turn the direction of conversation, or get away from the situation because we know we want God's best in our lives.

Here is an example of what that might look like:

Joe: Hey Dude! Long time no see!

Bill: Yeah, man! How've you been?

Joe: I'm good. I'm much better than Tom. I just found out he got audited by the IRS!

(Bill recognizes that Joe doesn't understand that gossip is harmful, so he takes the lead in walking in peace.)

Bill: Wow, man. That's too bad. Let's keep this quiet to preserve his reputation and pray for him. He would do the same for us.

(Bill immediately leads them in a short prayer for favor, wisdom, and help for Tom.)

If we turn every opportunity for gossip into an opportunity for prayer, those that only want to gossip will quit including us and those that really care for others will come to us first.

What if others are gossiping about us?

And keep a good conscience so that in the thing in which you are slandered, those who revile your good behavior in Christ will be put to shame. 1 Peter 3:16 (NASB)

But I say to you, love your enemies and pray for those who persecute you. Matt 5:44 (NASB)

We can't always help it if others want to spread untrue and malicious things about us. It can really hurt, especially if it is from a trusted friend or family member. God sees this and knows what we are going through, and as we lean into His complete acceptance and overflowing love for us through Christ, the sting of the gossip lessens, and His love towards others through us overwhelms the negative emotions we feel. Meditating on His great love for us is the best salve for our broken hearts, and because He loves us, we can then forgive and love others with His powerful, victorious love! Because He wins, we win!

Talebearing

Simply put, talebearing is when we tell a story that isn't ours to tell. Another term that might be more familiar is a "blabber-mouth." This is different from gossip or slander in that the story doesn't have to be negative or disparage another's character.

He that goeth about as a talebearer revealeth secrets: therefore meddle not with him that flattereth with his lips. Proverbs 20:19 (KJV)

For example, Sister Susie and her husband have been trying to have a baby for many years without success. One day, you bump into her and she is super excited and is bubbling with happiness. She tells you that she just got a report from her doctor that she is pregnant. This is joyous news and she runs off to tell her husband. You then proceed to tell all of your common friends about the glorious news without her permission. The first person you tell just happens to be at lunch with Susie's husband and immediately tells him. The surprise is ruined when Susie wanted to be the first to tell him, and now strife enters into your relationship with Susie.

This is very easy to get into, especially if it's good news like in this example. It will take some practice to learn the difference, but if we will pay attention to walking in the spirit, and the Holy Spirit Speed Bump, He will instruct us when not to speak.

> *Where no wood is, there the fire goeth out: so where there is no talebearer, the strife ceaseth. Proverbs 26:20 (KJV)*

One good rule of thumb is that we can share the news if it is officially on Facebook or Twitter, or another social media source—if it is common knowledge.

Purposefully walking in the spirit and in love will ensure we are avoiding all these baits and staying out of walking in the flesh. Sometimes we will fall into "autopilot," and take a bait because our mind is on the flesh. As soon as we see one of these baits manifesting in our lives, we need to immediately repent and submit to God again. We can use these baits as indicators that we need to shift our focus away from the mind on the flesh and back into walking in the spirit!

Lies:

1. It's harmless and doesn't actually hurt anyone if they don't know about it.

2. Listening to gossip about others helps me to pray for them.

Truth:

1. The Bible tells us that gossip brings strife between friends and God doesn't like that. (Proverbs 16:28)

2. Words of gossip will get down into your heart and affect how you treat that other person. Remember the vomit analogy? (Proverbs 18:8)

Questions

1. Is gossip, slander, or talebearing a challenge for you? If so, what lie are you believing?

_____

_____

_____

2. What are you going to do when someone else chooses to gossip in your presence? (Making a plan ahead of time will help you when you encounter this situation.)

_____

_____

_____

_____

_____

_____

_____

Prayer of Submission to avoid Gossip, Slander, and Talebearing and to trust God:

Wise and Good Father, I have not always kept my tongue from gossip, slander, or talebearing. Because of my own insecurity or pride, I have said things I shouldn't have, and have hurt the reputations of others because of my words. Please forgive me. Please show me where I need to change and give me the strength to do it! I choose to submit to Your will with my mouth. I choose to walk in the spirit and love with my every word. I choose to keep confidences. Thank You for the wisdom and ability to love with my words. Let my every word be like a gift of Your grace to everyone that hears me speak as I submit My thoughts and words to You. Hallelujah! Amen.

Now, pick ONE scripture from this chapter about Gossip, Slander, and Talebearing to put on a 3x5 card in your home to meditate on and memorize. This will help you avoid the lies and walk in the spirit, not in the flesh, in this area.

DEBATE

Now the deeds of the flesh are evident, which are: immorality, impurity, sensuality, idolatry, sorcery, enmities, strife, jealousy, outbursts of anger, disputes, dissensions, factions... Galatians 5:19-20 (NASB)

When a positive exchange of ideas and understanding turns negative—into an opportunity to assert one's own opinion and ideas over someone else's, debate has entered into the situation. Other translations of the same word in greek are: strifes, quarrels. rivalries, contentions, wrangling, enmities, and variances. Another word translated in the Bible as debate or strife also means factiousness, partisanship, and contention. These paint a picture of uncontrolled flesh running amok and spewing selfish pride into an otherwise healthy discussion. It is a sure sign of walking in the flesh and it leads to strife and death, yet again. Another word that is sometimes translated as contention, or wrangling, is found in 2 Timothy,

Remind them of these things, and solemnly charge them in the presence of God not to wrangle about words, which is useless and leads to the ruin of the hearers. Be diligent to present yourself approved to God as a workman who does not need to be ashamed, accurately handling the word of truth. But avoid worldly and empty chatter, for it will lead to further ungodliness, and their talk will spread like gangrene. 2 Timothy 2:14-17a (NASB)

God is always looking out for us. He knows that silly arguments about unimportant matters are harmful to us. Paul tells Timothy what will happen to those who debate and argue: it "leads to the ruin of the hearers." Wrangling, or disputing, over trifling matters attacks our faith in the Word of God by practicing doubt in what we hear. The Lord wants us to trust what He tells us, but if we are used to arguing with everything we hear, we won't be able to stop when it comes to the Word of God. Instead, God wants us to study His Word, believe it, and present ourselves approved to God as His ready and willing workman.

As a Christian, we may believe we have to defend the Word of God to everyone that would criticize it, or debate other Christians so they can see the error of their beliefs. Engaging in arguments over religious tenets of faith is actually counter-productive to peace and the work of the Holy Spirit. There is a time and a place where we can respectfully share what we believe the Word of God is telling us, but when a pleasant, peaceful conversation turns to an argument, we have turned our walk from the spirit to the flesh. A great scripture to meditate on, which shows what walking in the spirit in our conversation looks like, is found in James 3.

> But the wisdom from above is first pure [morally and spiritually undefiled], then peace-loving [courteous, considerate], gentle, reasonable [and willing to listen], full of compassion and good fruits. It is unwavering, without [self-righteous] hypocrisy [and self-serving guile]. And the seed whose fruit is righteousness (spiritual maturity) is sown in peace by those who make peace [by actively encouraging goodwill between individuals]. James 3:17-18 (AMP)

James is reminding us priorities are for peace first, before proving our points. When two sides are trying to defend themselves and their viewpoint, they are less likely to really listen to what the other side is saying—that's debate. When people aren't listening, they can't receive from the Lord.

The seed we sow as we choose peace first will produce the fruit of spiritual maturity in the minds and hearts of others. That's because the Holy Spirit can work so much better in an atmosphere of peace. As we are seeking peace and pursuing it—even in our desire to instruct others in the way of Christ—we are giving Him every avenue to speak to their hearts with conviction and encouragement in the truth. The Word says it's God's kindness that leads us to repentance (Romans 2:4), not His brow-beating us with how wrong we are!

> Knowledge puffs up, but love builds up. 1 Corinthians 8:1 (NIV-1984)

The opportunity to get into debate is going to happen. When it does, if we walk in love, we will value the opportunity to love this person over trying to be right and assert our knowledge. Sometimes, situations come along in which we can seek God's righteousness, or we can be right, but not both. It is the truth of God's love and grace on our lives that will ring true in people's hearts, not our trying to convince them we are right.

Are we allowed to talk about topics with others over which we may not agree? Honest discussion can be very fruitful and educational, but the moment emotions become strong, or we sense strife entering into the discussion, we must STOP!!!! We have to walk in the spirit, and trust God to lead us into peace in these things if we don't want to walk in the flesh and reap broken relationships. If we must continue the exchange, we need to let feelings fade, or simply agree to disagree. By doing this, we are doing what God commands us to do in Ephesians 4:3,

> *being diligent to preserve the unity of the Spirit in the bond of peace. (NASB)*

Obeying God's Word always brings good fruit!

Don't Be a Sucker! Don't Make the Trade!

A "sucker" is someone who can be easily cheated out of something, or easily deceived. Nobody wants to be a "sucker," but the enemy's main goal in life is to get us to sign up to be one. How do we become a sucker? By being critical, judgmental, gossiping, talebearing, taking offense, holding unforgiveness, debating, worrying, or being jealous. These are all works of the flesh and will all produce death in our lives. If the enemy can deceive us into one of these behaviors, he has gotten us into the flesh, and can steal our peace in the meantime, turning us into a sucker.

Think about it—what do we really get in exchange for being critical of someone? Or debating about the current political leadership? Nothing. That's a bad deal! Don't make the trade. Don't be a sucker. Let's keep our mouth shut if we need to, renew our thinking with God's Word, and pray for God to help us see that other person the way He does, and then we will walk in a powerful peace.

One last thing about all the baits

We have spent the last few chapters diving deeper into what the baits are, how they work on us, and how walking in the spirit will help us avoid them. Satan uses these baits to try and attack our lives every day. When we go on autopilot emotionally, and quit listening to our spirit man and the Holy Spirit, we become victims of these baits and our lives become filled with strife, confusion, and chaos.

Lies:

1. God expects me to explain the error of someone else's beliefs.

2. Peace isn't as important as showing someone how they are wrong.

Truth:

1. Actually, what God expects of us is to love others. Sometimes we get to share God's Word with them, but love and peace are always our first priority. (Romans 13:8)

2. Seeking peace first is the best way for God to be able to use us to share His truth with others. (James 3:17-18)

Questions

1. Is there a particular topic that you struggle to discuss without getting into strife with those that disagree with you?

How does debate negatively affect our witness for Christ?

_____

_____

_____

_____

_____

_____

_____

2. How does debate negatively affect our fellowship with other believers?

_____

_____

_____

_____

_____

_____

_____

Prayer of Submission to avoid Debate and to walk in the spirit:

Peaceful and Holy Father, You desire for all of Your children to walk in peace together and in unity. Debating with each other takes us right out of that place of powerful peace. I'm sorry I have engaged in fruitless and silly arguments that led to the ruin of myself and those that heard me. Please forgive me. By Your Spirit in my heart, I will choose to walk in peace instead of trying to assert my own opinions about things. Doing things Your way is always the better way. I choose to walk in the spirit, in peace, and in love. Thank You for the wisdom and strength to do it! Hallelujah! Amen.

Now, pick ONE scripture from this chapter about Debate to put on a 3x5 card in your home to meditate on and memorize. This will help you avoid the lies and walk in the spirit, not in the flesh, in this area.

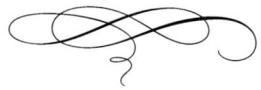

THE POWER OF UNITY

Therefore if there is any encouragement in Christ, if there is any consolation of love, if there is any fellowship of the Spirit, if any affection and compassion, make my joy complete by being of the same mind, maintaining the same love, united in spirit, intent on one purpose. Philippians 2:1-2 (NASB)

Up to this point in the study we have spent our time defining peace, exploring God's best for our lives, and exposing the baits the enemy uses to get us out from under the peace of Christ, which we have as we walk in the spirit and in love. Another powerful characteristic of God's peace is the power of unity with those around us. At the base of the word "unity" is the prefix "uni," which means "one." When we are united in one purpose, one heart, and one action with those around us, the sum of the accomplishments is greater than the sum of its parts, and the enemy knows this.

Unity in the World

The reason the enemy tries so hard to keep Christians out of the peace of God and peace with each other is that there is so much power released when there is a spirit of unity. There is something that goes on supernaturally, when any group of people comes together for a common purpose and disregard their differences. Let's take a look at the Tower of Babel.

*Now the whole earth used the same language and the same words.
It came about as they journeyed east, that they found a plain in the
land of Shinar and settled there. They said to one another, "Come, let
us make bricks and burn them thoroughly." And they used brick for
stone, and they used tar for mortar. They said, "Come, let us build for
ourselves a city, and a tower whose top will reach into heaven, and let
us make for ourselves a name, otherwise we will be scattered abroad
over the face of the whole earth." Genesis 11:1-4 (NASB)*

We can see here that the people of Babel "used the same language and the same words," in other words, they were united as a country or a body of people in their language and mindset. They traveled together and were united in the purpose of building a city for their own glory, directly challenging the authority of God in their lives. God told humanity to "Be fruitful and multiply, and fill the earth, and subdue it" in Genesis 1:28. This is actually the first command recorded in the Bible that God gave to man. The people of Babel purposely decided to follow their own agenda instead of the purposes and will of God, and created a monument to themselves and their own ability. They chose to stay all together in one place and glorify themselves in their works. In verses 5 and 6, we see

*The LORD came down to see the city and the tower which the sons
of men had built. The LORD said, "Behold, they are one people, and
they all have the same language. And this is what they began to
do, and now nothing which they purpose to do will be impossible for
them." Genesis 11:5-6 (NASB)*

God notes here that the people of Babel were "one people" and all spoke the same tongue and had a united purpose. Because of this unity, He stated that "nothing which they purpose to do will be impossible for them."

This unity was simply a result of people coming together for a common purpose, and didn't even include unity with God and His will. The people of Babel just had a common goal and were working together, united, to accomplish it.

But God had to destroy the tower and scatter the people because their desires were incongruent with His plans for mankind. He wanted to restore His broken relationship with man. He wanted to bless mankind, but as long as they were looking to themselves and each other for fulfillment, they were going to come up empty. Man cannot fill the deepest desires in his heart for purpose and love. Only God's presence can do that.

Unity in the Church

There has been division across racial and religious lines since the time of the Tower of Babel. God wants us to walk in unity with each other in the right way, by using our unity to love one another as He loves us. The death and resurrection of Christ serves as a bridge between not only God and man, but man and man as well. We see in Ephesians 2,

> *For He Himself is our peace, who made both groups into one and broke down the barrier of the dividing wall, by abolishing in His flesh the enmity, which is the Law of commandments contained in ordinances, so that in Himself He might make the two into one new man, thus establishing peace, and might reconcile them both in one body to God through the cross, by it having put to death the enmity. Ephesians 2:14-16 (NASB)*

Jesus reconciled Jews and Gentiles on the cross, and created "one new man, thus establishing peace." There no longer needs to be division in the Body of Christ—the church—at all because the cross has "put to death the enmity." We can see this clearly in another group of people who were walking in the power of unity and seeing some incredible results because of it. In Acts chapter 2, we see the birth of the modern Christian church body as the baptism of the Holy Spirit is poured out on the day of Pentecost.

According to the book of Acts, the apostles and other believers, totaling about 120, were instructed by Christ to wait in Jerusalem until they received power from on high. When the day of Pentecost, a Jewish holiday celebrating the giving of the law on Mount Sinai, arrived, they were all filled with the Holy Spirit and spoke with other tongues, i.e. various languages. Acts 2:5-6 continues the story,

> *Now there were Jews living in Jerusalem, devout men from every nation under heaven. And when this sound occurred, the crowd came together, and were bewildered because each one of them was hearing them [the disciples] speak in his own language. (NASB)*

We can see here that the gift of the Holy Spirit enabled the foreigners to understand the Jewish believers! It goes on to say in verse 11 that the foreigners exclaim, "we hear them in our own tongues speaking of the mighty deeds of God!" The Apostle Peter then speaks to the gathering crowd and shares the plan of salvation through Jesus Christ. Three thousand souls are added to the Church that day! The believers continued in a spirit of unity, and God was able to work many miracles and add many souls to the Body of Christ as a result.

> *Everyone kept feeling a sense of awe; and many wonders and signs were taking place through the apostles. And all those who had believed were together and had all things in common; and they began selling their property and possessions and were sharing them with all, as anyone might have need. Day by day continuing with one mind in the temple, and breaking bread from house to house, they were taking their meals together with gladness and sincerity of heart, praising God and having favor with all the people. And the Lord was adding to their number day by day those who were being saved. Acts 2:43-47 (NASB)*

Imagine what can be done in the local church when we not only walk in unity with God and His purposes, but are also determined to stay out of strife with one another and walk in unity with our fellow Christians, regardless of denomination, race, creed, or background. The church in Acts walked in abundance of signs and wonders, provision, fellowship, and favor, and the "Lord was adding to their number day by day those who were being saved!" There was such a spirit of unity and fellowship, the church was increasing DAILY!

There is great power released when a body of people, even nonbelievers, choose to be united in message and purpose and simply put the goals and agenda of the group above divisive personal opinions. When this body of people are believers, with the baptism of the Holy Spirit, and are submitted to God in all ways, supernatural and miraculous things will happen! We can truly have His kingdom come and His will be done on Earth as it is in Heaven! (Matthew 6:10)

Unity in Prayer

In Matthew 18:19-20, Jesus gives us some very powerful promises. He says,

> *Again I say to you, that if two of you agree on earth about anything that they may ask, it shall be done for them by My Father who is in heaven. For where two or three have gathered together in My name, I am there in their midst. (NASB)*

We have used these verses time and again to obtain God's best for our lives. Jesus is giving us the promise of ANYTHING, and the only requirements are that two of us agree on earth and that we ask! This is sometimes called the "prayer of agreement," and is a powerful tool given to us by Jesus to see God's will done in our lives. We have found that it takes the power of the Holy Spirit to continually remain in agreement with someone else over an issue. It seems that our flesh will want its own way, and will not be able to work with other believers in unity if not under subjection to the Holy Spirit. This is a great way to be sure we are walking in the spirit, and praying according to the will of God, and we know we will have whatever we ask for (1 John 5:14). We can also be led by the peace of God when we are asking for something. Romans 8:6 says, "For the mind set on the flesh is death, but the mind set on the Spirit is life and peace (NASB)." When we are led by peace, we know that our mind is set on the Spirit instead of the flesh, and we are praying according to the will of God.

Here is how we apply the prayer of agreement in our lives:

1. Define a need or prayer point.

2. Find out God's will on the subject through His word and prayer.

3. Find someone with whom you can agree in prayer (spouse, good friend, pastor) and stay in agreement with them.

4. Pray and agree that the request is answered.

5. When ever the topic comes up again, thank God for His provision.

> Greg and I have a scrapbook at home filled with answered prayers and miracles that God has done in our lives. We call it our "Glory Book" because it recounts in detail many glorious things our loving Heavenly Father has done for us. It causes us to give Him praise and honor and glory every time we get it out! The prayer of agreement is one of the many tools we used in some of the most amazing miracles in our Glory Book, and we have seen it work time and time again as we chose to walk in love and peace and stay in unity! —Sharon

Walking in Unity

Can two walk together, unless they are agreed?– Amos 3:3 (KJV)

We have presented the idea of unity, but how do we practically walk in unity with others? Simply by considering the goals which we are pursuing. Unity is usually dispersed when there are multiple agendas. There will be times when what we want and what the other person wants will be in contention. When that happens, we will need to decide what's more important: getting what we want, or choosing to have faith in God that our needs will be met, and instead lifting up the agenda of another person.

Beyond all these things put on love, which is the perfect bond of unity. Colossians 3:14 (NASB)

Maintaining our love walk is the key to getting and keeping true unity between believers. When we stop seeking our own ways and start seeking to bless and love others, unity will be the natural by-product.

Final Thought

All of us are called by God to be an important part of His work on the earth. Ephesians 2:10 states that "we are God's workmanship, created in Christ Jesus to do good works, which God prepared in advance for us to do." (NIV-1984) We all have different purposes and callings, but all of us are integral to the proper working of the body of Christ (1 Corinthians 12:27).

When we let our flesh rule and strife comes in to our lives, it interrupts and thwarts the ministry we are called in to. If we become distracted by criticism or judgment, we become ineffective and useless. When we walk in the spirit we will remain in peace, our callings will become evident to us and others, and our ministries and purposes will flourish.

1. Pick one of your relationships that would benefit from deeper levels of unity. Find out what the other person's goals/desires are and write them down.

_____

_____

_____

_____

_____

2. Think of one or two things you can do to help the person in question #1 achieve their goals.

_____

_____

_____

_____

_____

PEACEFUL WARFARE

Fight the good fight of faith; take hold of the eternal life to which you were called, and you made the good confession in the presence of many witnesses. 1 Timothy 6:13 (NASB)

We have briefly identified some of the pitfalls of walking in the flesh that the enemy will place in our path, as well as God's way to victory. This amounts to a lifestyle of warfare to keep the powerful peace of God in the forefront of our lives. When we say warfare, we mean a conscious effort on our part to guard against the enemy and his attempts to sidetrack us with his agenda, which is this: **to get us away from focusing on walking in the spirit and love and achieving God's will for our lives.** If he can do that, it can not only affect our lives, but also the lives of the people God wants us to reach out to and touch for Him. Being used by God to help others is one of the most important purposes for our lives. The enemy knows this, and if he can derail us with strife, he makes us ineffective. There are lives tied to our obedience to walk in the spirit.

The only thing the devil can do is convince us to lay down our peace and get into strife. He does this by lying and deceiving us into taking one of the baits. We have nothing to fear from our enemy. He has no power on his own to prevent us from accomplishing God's will.

When He had disarmed the rulers and authorities, He made a public display of them, having triumphed over them through Him. Colossians 2:15 (NASB)

God made a "public spectacle" of the devil by triumphing over him with the cross. The love of God was on clear display! Unfortunately, Satan isn't going to quit trying to thwart God's plans for us. Let's discuss the warfare of peace, its battlegrounds, and the weapons God has provided for us.

No Auto-Pilot

Be sober, be vigilant; because your adversary the devil, as a roaring lion, walketh about, seeking whom he may devour: 1 Peter 5:8 (KJV)

For we wrestle not against flesh and blood, but against principalities, against powers, against the rulers of the darkness of this world, against spiritual wickedness in high places. Ephesians 6:12 (KJV)

These scriptures remind us that people are not our problem, the devil is. They demonstrate how dangerous he can be, and that we should be on the lookout for him in regards to the peace in our lives. We use the term "no auto-pilot" to refer to the act of consciously paying attention to our surroundings, what we are thinking, where those thoughts are coming from, and what we are sensing. If we don't, the devil has a free ride to distract and deceive us. If we are not paying attention, he can get us to put our trust in our emotions and our limited understanding, which are easily manipulated. It doesn't take much to get us into strife if we are on "auto-pilot." The devil uses strife very shrewdly to short circuit our effectiveness in the lives of others. He doesn't want us to walk around and change lives like Jesus did.

One evening, after my job delivering pizzas all afternoon, I decided to go to a self-serve car wash and wash my car. It was one of those coin-operated car washes with the wands that shoot high pressure water and soap out. As I was rinsing my car, an elderly woman walked by the other end of the bay and I heard the thoughts, "You want to spray that old woman with water." The Lord gave me discernment to realize that idea hadn't come from me! The devil was trying to make me think I wanted to spray her! Immediately after that, I heard, "You are such a lousy Christian! You wanted to spray that elderly lady with water! You should be ashamed!" I instantly recognized this time where the thoughts were coming from! The enemy was trying to condemn me for thoughts that HE had planted in my head in the first place! It was a great lesson for me to see that some of the temptations and thoughts that are contrary to the Word of God, don't even originate from our own thinking! I'm not saying that all evil thoughts are from the devil, however. The Bible teaches us that evil thoughts come out of the unrenewed heart of man (Mark 7:21), but the Word of God also shows us in Luke 4:2 that temptation can come from the devil. When thoughts of judgment and criticism of others or ourselves come into our minds, we need to remember that they may be baits from the devil to ensnare us and get us off track! Wherever these strifeful thoughts are from, our response is the same. Submit to God, resist, and get back into peace! —Sharon

The devil will try and deceive us into believing that he is not involved at all in our conflicts and that if our circumstances or present company would change, we could be at peace.

If the devil can convince us with his lies that the "other" person is really our problem, he has us beaten already. When we come to our senses and see what is really going on, we can face our enemy head-on and resist him in faith, knowing that God has given us everything we need to be successful in this life (2 Peter 1:3).

The following illustrations show the difference between being a sucker, and walking vigilantly in the spirit and peace on purpose.

The Devil gets us to blame each other

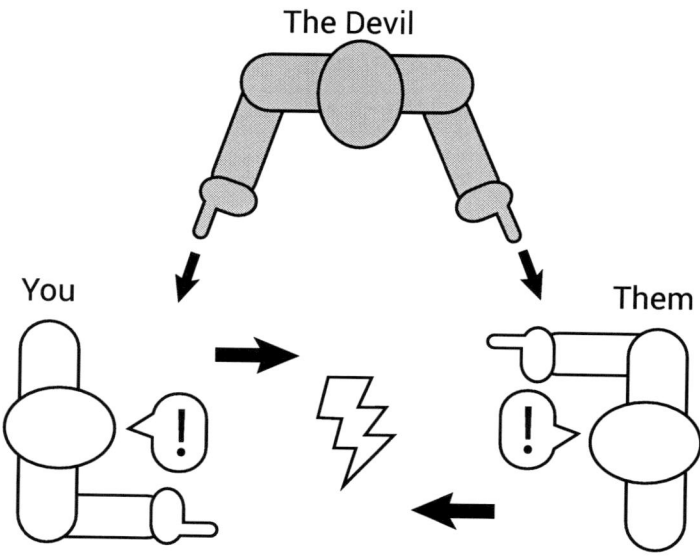

The devil will try and get us to criticize and judge one another and forget who the real enemy is: him!

Unite against your real enemy, the Devil

We must choose to recognize that the devil is the enemy and the accuser of the brethren (Rev 12:10). Instead of verbalizing the thoughts and emotions that the devil is trying to get us to use on each other, choose to unite, turn, and defeat the enemy with the Word of God and His promises!

As we continue walking in the love and peace of God, the Holy Spirit is able to steer us clear of strife-filled situations, and also give us wisdom to walk through the situations we simply cannot avoid. This greatly helps us to be able to walk in victory in all areas because we hear God's wisdom in the affairs of life and follow His directions. We aren't so distracted by the things that have no lasting importance. As we engaged in the battles of our lives, here are four key strategies we found in scripture and through experience.

Submitting to God

Therefore submit to God. Resist the devil and he will flee from you.
James 4:7 (NKJV)

This may seem like a "no-brainer," but if we try and take authority over the devil and resist him, but haven't taken the time to be submitted to God, we will fail—every time. It is not our authority that the devil flees from, but God's. Whenever we find ourselves powerless over the enemy, we need to check on our obedience walk and make sure we haven't disobeyed in an area. This can even include procrastination to do the right thing. Delayed obedience is still disobedience. A great example of this occurred in the book of Acts as a group of Jews went around driving out evil spirits from people.

Some Jews who went around driving out evil spirits tried to invoke the name of the Lord Jesus over those who were demon-possessed. They would say, "In the name of the Jesus whom Paul preaches, I command you to come out." Seven sons of Sceva, a Jewish chief priest, were doing this. One day the evil spirit answered them, "Jesus I know, and Paul I know about, but who are you?" Then the man who had the evil spirit jumped on them and overpowered them all. He gave them such a beating that they ran out of the house naked and bleeding. Acts 19:13-16 (NIV)

These disciples of Sceva were trying to invoke authority of a name they hadn't submitted to, and subsequently got the beating of their lives! We have to be submitted to what God has told us to do if we want to be effective in walking in His authority.

Submission starts with right thinking. Our thought life is the primary battlefield on which the warfare of peace takes place. The opportunities to walk in the flesh and give up our peace will come to us daily. The enemy will bring up old familiar temptations that have worked on us in the past. When we abide in His Presence, we can keep our thoughts and words in line with the Word of God, and we will be much more likely to promptly obey the leading of the Holy Spirit regarding any issue. 2 Corinthians 10:5 says,

> *"We are destroying speculations and every lofty thing raised up against the knowledge of God, and we are taking every thought captive to the obedience of Christ" (NASB).*

We see here that even our thoughts must be taken captive by us and directed into obedience to Christ.

Our feelings must also be submitted to the Word of God. Our whole lives the world teaches us that our feelings and emotions are some supernatural 6th sense that can give us special insight into our lives and the lives of those around us. While feelings are a gift from God and a good thing, they do not provide peace and direction. Feelings are a by-product of what we are believing and thinking, and so more consideration should be given to what we are believing and thinking than to how we feel. As we saw earlier, we are to take our thoughts captive and submit them to approval by God. This is a critical step in the "seek peace and pursue it" discipline.

When we feel depressed or unsatisfied, we can make the decision to start being thankful. We submit to God by following His encouragement to rejoice and be thankful, even when we don't want to. We may not "feel" like doing it, but this is a good example of how putting our faith in the truth of God's Word can change our feelings. Dare to speak out loud 20 things about which you are thankful to God at that moment you notice you are "down." After you have done it, take a self-assessment on how you "feel." You won't be in the same place emotionally, and thankfulness is the key. We can continue to be thankful and verbally praise God for what He has done in our lives. This purposeful act of our will changes our feelings and attitudes and rescues us from the negative emotions that can try to control us.

One Saturday morning, as I was watching my two younger sons take swimming lessons, I had myself a good ol' fashioned pity party. I had been thinking about how much I had to do as a mother of four children, how I was unable to keep up with the housework, laundry, cooking, and cleaning all by myself. My computer was messed up, my extended family was mad at me, and I wasn't too pleased with myself either! I am sure I was nursing some anger or frustration with Greg for saying or doing something that offended me (real or imagined!) I was feeling pretty low! I started texting Greg about how rotten I was feeling and he challenged me to be thankful instead of focusing on the negative. I had to decide if I really did want victory and joy and peace, or if I just wanted someone to come along side and say, "poor baby!" Thankfully, Greg doesn't do "poor baby" with me, and he won't indulge my self-pity. He charged me to start listing my blessings. I texted him that I was thankful the boys were doing well in swimming lessons. He encouraged me to think of more. I answered with a few more things. He wanted more still! I listed a few more things, then I noticed I wasn't feeling quite so heavy. My flesh was still drawn to complaining and whining, but I could sense that my spirit was being revived as I turned my thoughts away from myself and the flesh(death) and onto the spirit and the blessings He had provided me. After another dozen blessings, I was getting downright giddy! Thankfulness changes us! Isaiah 61:3 states that Jesus was anointed to give us "the garment of praise for the spirit of heaviness." So when you find yourself down and out, look up! He has given you SOOOO much to be thankful for, and remembering those things can change your perspective and attitude! —Sharon

1. Let's take a moment to make "submitting to God" more personal. Think of a situation in which you need God's supernatural intervention. How would "submitting to God" look in that situation?

_____

_____

_____

Holding Our Peace

As we are walking in love and the spirit, we are submitted to God and His way of doing things in our situation, and we can expect Him to show up on our behalf and bring about victory!

As Moses led the children of Israel out of slavery in Egypt, the Egyptians changed their minds and wanted their slaves back. They start chasing the Israelites into the desert to recapture and take them back to bondage in Egypt. (There's a great lesson to us here about how the devil will try to drag us back into our old areas of bondage after our salvation!) The Israelites were understandably dismayed and cried out to the Lord and to Moses.

> *And Moses said to the people, "Do not be afraid. Stand still, and see the salvation of the Lord, which He will accomplish for you today. For the Egyptians whom you see today, you shall see again no more forever. The Lord will fight for you, and you shall hold your peace."*
> *Exodus 14:13–14 (NKJV)*

Holding our peace and letting God fight our battles for us not only ensures our victory, but it brings us closer to Him as we see His true character and love for us. 1 Peter 5:7 says that we can be

> *Casting the whole of your care [all your anxieties, all your worries, all your concerns, once and for all] on Him, for He cares for you affectionately and cares about you watchfully. (AMP)*

If the devil can get us out of peace by our circumstances, he is in control. He may bring storms and challenges into our lives, but he has no control over us unless we give up our peace and give in to worry and self-care. God wants us to rest in the midst of the storms of life, knowing that He loves us and is taking care of us.

Mark 4:35-41 shares the story of when Christ was asleep on the stern of the boat crossing the Sea of Galilee.

> *On that day, when evening came, He said to them, "Let us go over to the other side." Leaving the crowd, they took Him along with them in the boat, just as He was; and other boats were with Him. And there arose a fierce gale of wind, and the waves were breaking over the boat so much that the boat was already filling up. Jesus Himself was in the stern, asleep on the cushion; and they woke Him and said to Him,*

"Teacher, do You not care that we are perishing?" And He got up and rebuked the wind and said to the sea, "Hush, be still." And the wind died down and it became perfectly calm. And He said to them, " Why are you afraid? Do you still have no faith?" They became very much afraid and said to one another, "Who then is this, that even the wind and the sea obey Him?" (NASB)

Let's take a moment and ask some hypothetical questions. If the disciples had not bothered to wake Jesus, what would have happened to the boat and the people on it? Would God have allowed Jesus to perish in the sea? Certainly not! So were they really in any danger? Logic would dictate that they were not going to die and thus were in fear for no reason. We never have to fear in any circumstance. We can rest, knowing that God has us in the palm of His hand, and that we are protected and provided for.

When we rest in Him and trust Him to lead us to victory, we are giving over control of the situation to Him. We are, in a sense, giving Him the reins of our lives, and are submitting to His authority. When we do this, we can be sure He will carry us to the other side of the seas of our lives, regardless of whatever storms arise. We also see this illustrated when the children of Israel came to the city of Jericho, on their march to take over the Promised Land, in Joshua 6.

Now Jericho was tightly shut because of the sons of Israel; no one went out and no one came in. The LORD said to Joshua, "See, I have given Jericho into your hand, with its king and the valiant warriors. You shall march around the city, all the men of war circling the city once. You shall do so for six days. Also seven priests shall carry seven trumpets of rams' horns before the ark; then on the seventh day you shall march around the city seven times, and the priests shall blow the trumpets. It shall be that when they make a long blast with the ram's horn, and when you hear the sound of the trumpet, all the people shall shout with a great shout; and the wall of the city will fall down flat, and the people will go up every man straight ahead." Joshua 6:1-5 (NASB)

Here, we see the children of Israel were walking in obedience to what God had told them to do, even though it didn't make any sense in the natural world. They were just to walk around Jericho for 7 days and give a great shout! Not only did God bring about a great victory for the Israelites after their obedience, but the city wall fell down flat. The people could just walk straight into the city, without having to climb over all the torn down walls! Archaeological digs have verified the truth of this account as scientists have found the walls were knocked all the way down flat.[6]

2. Let's take a moment to make "holding your peace" more personal in the situation you used in the previous exercise. How would "holding your peace" look in that situation?

_____

_____

_____

_____

When we hold our peace, it is a sure sign of our victory from God and our enemy's defeat . Philippians 1:28 in the Amplified Bible states,

> *And do not [for a moment] be frightened or intimidated in anything by your opponents and adversaries, for such [constancy and fearlessness] will be a clear sign (proof and seal) to them of [their impending] destruction, but [a sure token and evidence] of your deliverance and salvation, and that from God. (AMP)*

Speaking God's Word

When God created the heavens and the earth, He spoke out loud, saying, "Let there be light" and "Let dry land appear" (Genesis 1). God created us in His image, so we can use His words to create what He has promised by speaking His Word into any situation. In the book of James, we learn that the tongue controls the direction of the man.

> *For we all stumble in many things. If anyone does not stumble in word, he is a perfect man, able also to bridle the whole body. Indeed, we put bits in horses' mouths that they may obey us, and we turn their whole body. Look also at ships: although they are so large and are driven by fierce winds, they are turned by a very small rudder wherever the pilot desires. James 3:2-4 (NKJV)*

Speaking God's Word out loud is also a way of submitting to God's will in our lives.

Just as the bit and bridle control the horse, so our tongue controls our direction. When we are speaking God's Word out loud, we are giving Him direct control over our direction and destination.

In Matthew 4, we have one of the accounts of the temptation of Christ in the wilderness. He had been fasting for 40 days and became hungry. He was then tempted by the devil to get into worry and self-care, and meet His own needs by His own hands and turn stones into bread. Sometimes, if God's provision doesn't come in the time frame we think we must meet, we seek to satisfy our needs by our own hand. Evidently Jesus could have done this miracle, or it wouldn't have been a real temptation for Him; but, Jesus knew to keep trusting in the provision of His Father, even if it was taking longer than His flesh would have liked. When Jesus, who is our best example, faced the enemy in the wilderness, He answered temptation with God's Word, and spoke words of trust in His Father. We are following His example when we answer the temptations we encounter with His Word.

God's Word is our guide and insight into His will, and can shed light into any situation. Knowing the Word gives the Holy Spirit resources to use in our lives,— it renews our minds and changes us from the inside. When we are in a situation where we are being tempted by the enemy to lose our peace, the Holy Spirit will bring His Word to our remembrance. 1 Corinthians 10:13 says,

> *No temptation has seized you except what is common to man. And God is faithful; he will not let you be tempted beyond what you can bear. But when you are tempted, he will also provide a way out so that you can stand up under it. (NIV)*

Learning to listen to God when we are being tempted or in an argument will bring about the peace and resolution we are wanting. He will tell us when to speak and when to stop speaking using the Holy Spirit speed bump we talked about in Chapter Three. This is true spiritual warfare, and can change a situation and protect us from the enemy's advances.

3. Let's take a moment to make "speaking God's Word" more personal in the situation you used in the previous exercise. How would "speaking God's Word" look in that situation?

_____

_____

Walking in Love

When we choose to walk in love with someone else, it is a conscious act of powerful warfare.

Above all, keep fervent in your love for one another, because love covers a multitude of sins. 1 Peter 4:8 (NKJV)

When we are walking in love, we are choosing to preserve and protect our relationships instead of being concerned with justice for ourselves when we are wronged. If we will choose to walk in love with others, we will stay in peace, and God can use us to minister His love and freedom. Remember, "Love never fails!"

Just for That!

As we choose walking in the spirit as our lifestyle, we will start doing "strange" things in the natural. There are definitely seasons of testing we go through from time to time, and walking in love will lead us to victory. Sharon and I have adopted a strategy that turns our defensive posture into an offensive posture. Here is how it works: let's say that the devil is battling against us in our thought life trying to get us to be critical or judgmental against someone in our life. When we realize what's really going on, we say, "Just for that... I'm gonna..." and think of something to do for someone else, or something we can give to someone else that will cost us something and bring praise and honor to God! It's a great way to "overcome evil with good!" (Romans 12:21)

For example, there was a season when I was having a terrible time struggling with my attitude about a church I was attending. I disagreed with how some things were being done and I suddenly realized that the devil had lied to me about something related to my situation and I had believed it and acted on it, sending myself into strife. I repented of getting into strife using James 4:7, submitted to God, and told the devil to go away, but I wanted to do more. So I pulled out a "Just for that..." and made a donation to my church of something that meant a lot to me. This cost me in the natural, but that was the main point. I wanted to stick it to the devil and do something that expanded the Kingdom of God. This act was a conscious effort to let him know that if he messes with me, it's going to cost him, and expand God's blessings to others. —Greg

Peaceful Wartime Strategies

What do we do when we find ourselves in potential minefields of strife with others? Here are some practical ideas we have found to be effective in our war to keep our peace.

- Walk in the Spirit. (Galatians 5:16)
- Pray under your breath. (Matthew 5:43-45 (NASB))
- Say a quick prayer of "Help!" to God. This is surprisingly effective if you don't have time to or can't muster up a prayer with specifics. God knows what your heart is saying.
- Excuse yourself to the bathroom, and then seek God while you are there.
- Change the subject away from the topic that is strifeful.
- Stay out of criticism of the other person. Instead, find something worthy of praise to concentrate on.
- Privately speak the word of God over a situation, before the situation comes up if possible.
- We highly recommend a book called *Prayers That Avail Much* by Germaine Copeland to help you learn how to pray God's Word. It is also a great Bible study aid.
- Before you go into a possible strife-filled situation, pray over yourself and your family that you would walk in peace and love, etc.
- Don't make it worse. Bite your tongue if you have to, just don't do or say anything that make it worse.

Conclusions

The warfare of peace is a tool that enables us to stand up and have victory in our lives. No longer do we have to be powerless and helplessly take what comes at us, but we do have a responsibility to stand up and use these tools to bring the kingdom of God and His freedom to those in our lives.

> *From the days of John the Baptist until now the kingdom of heaven suffers violence, and violent men take it by force. Matthew 11:12 (NASB)*

No matter what other people choose to do, say or believe, we can be at peace with them. They may not reciprocate that peace to us, but our source is from God and God will work on our behalf. We have to keep resting in Jesus as our #1 priority, knowing He loves us, and abiding in His Presence. This will fuel our desire to do what it takes to reach beyond our mind set on the flesh, take hold of God's will, and resist the enemy's ploys.

4. List out some situations you already know about where you need to be more proactive in regards to preparing for warfare. Remember that people are not the problem—it's the devil that brings strife through others. You can prepare spiritually before you come into these situations IF you are not on "auto-pilot."

_____

_____

_____

_____

_____

_____

PEACE WITH GOD

Therefore, having been justified by faith, we have peace with God through our Lord Jesus Christ, Romans 5:1 (NASB)

When we asked God to forgive us of our sins and Jesus to come into our life, the ability for us and our Heavenly Father to have a relationship was established by removing the separation that sin had put between us and Him. Thank you Jesus for this! Hallelujah! Now that this separation has been bridged and forever sealed, we have to move into developing a healthy relationship with God based on the truth of His Word.

To completely enjoy the fullness of the relationship that Jesus paid for us to have, we have to renew our understanding about who God is, who we are to Him, and what He has done for us in Christ. This is because we have such a limited understanding of these things when we are first born again. Until that point, our knowledge of our Heavenly Father was based on things like what others had taught us (right or wrong), how our earthly parents treated us, and our own human reasoning. We can now experience a deeper sense of the peace of God as we grow in our knowledge of the Word, and dispel the lies we have believed about our Heavenly Father.

Understanding the Foundation of Our Peace

Grace and peace be multiplied to you in the knowledge of God and of Jesus our Lord; seeing that His divine power has granted to us everything pertaining to life and godliness, through the true knowledge of Him who called us by His own glory and excellence. 2 Peter 1:2-3 (NASB)

The foundation of our peace with God comes from a real understanding of His love toward us. Knowing we are loved and accepted by God helps us to love Him and to love ourselves, which is the foundation of our love for others. Ephesians 1:6 states that "He has made us accepted in the Beloved." God reconciled us to Himself in Christ, the Beloved. John 17:23 shows us that the Father loves us as He loved Jesus Himself! Wow! Knowing these truths and meditating on them will make them real in our lives and hearts and will change us from the inside out!

What we believe about our salvation determines how we relate to God. We don't end up experiencing peace with God and all the blessing that it brings on a daily basis until we understand what salvation does for us and how much our Heavenly Father really loves us! How did we get this peace with God in the first place?

> *The chastisement [needful to obtain] peace and well-being for us was upon Him... Isaiah 53:5 (AMP)*

Peace with God has been completely purchased for us because Jesus went to the cross on our behalf and paid for it ALL—past, present, and future! When we really believe that, we will run to Him even in the midst of our sin. We tend to believe that as long as we stay out of "major" sin, try to always obey, spend enough time with God during our quiet time, read enough of the Bible, etc., He is happy with us and we have peace with Him. Actually, we can never be "good enough" to qualify for His peace on our own merit. Paul addresses this in the book of Galatians when he writes,

> *Nevertheless knowing that a man is not justified by the works of the Law but through faith in Christ Jesus, even we have believed in Christ Jesus, so that we may be justified by faith in Christ and not by the works of the Law; since by the works of the Law no flesh will be justified. Galatians 2:16 (NASB)*

We see here that even Paul did not consider his own ministry to be anything that would justify him before God, but completely trusted in the work accomplished by Christ at the cross as his justification.

The response Adam had toward God after he sinned is totally different from the experience the believer now has in Christ. When Adam sensed God's presence in the Garden of Eden, he fled from God because he felt guilty and condemned. He had a sin-debt he was conscious of that caused him to flee from the presence of his best friend. Christ paid the debt for all our sins, so if we find ourselves afraid to come to our Heavenly Father, it's not from God, but from guilt and condemnation which no longer belong to us in Christ! (Romans 8:1) Now, because we have eternal peace with God, we can

> *Draw near with confidence to the throne of grace, so that we may receive mercy and find grace to help in time of need. Hebrews 4:16 (NASB)*

We no longer need to cower in fear of punishment when we come into our Father's Presence. We can now approach with confidence, knowing that all our sins are covered and He sees us with eyes of mercy and grace to help in our time of need--even in the very midst of our sins! Let's face it, we may need His help more when we are dealing with sin than at any other time in our daily lives. Our enemy would have us believe that our Father wants nothing to do with us during those times, but that is a lie! The truth is that He wants to help us out and bless us with wisdom and freedom at all times. The next time you are dealing with sin, in the very midst of it, call on Jesus and find Him ever ready to help and deliver you!

Taking a Bait with God

We can take the enemy's bait in our relationship toward our Heavenly Father, the same way we can take the bait in our relationships with others. We deal with unforgiveness toward God when He doesn't meet our expectations. We deal with criticism toward God when we don't like what He is or isn't doing. We deal with judgment when we have a negative opinion about or try to figure out why God does what He does. We can even worry in our relationship with God when we don't trust Him to lead us or keep us safe. We will be much happier when we let Him be the potter and remember we are the clay (Isaiah 29:16). This is so much easier when we know how much He loves us. Everything He brings us to or through is out of His heart of love for us. Not everything we go through is from Him; but He wants to lead us to victory in every challenge (Romans 8:28).

1. In what area in your life have you taken a bait with God?

_____

_____

_____

We aren't going to be able to enjoy peace with God until we trust Him. We will always be trying to take control back from His Hands because we don't believe He has our best interests at heart. If we find ourselves trying to control our circumstances, or control other people in our lives so we don't get hurt, or so that nothing bad happens to us or to someone we love, we are in fear and aren't trusting God with these things. When we have the revelation that He really loves us, we will find our fear fading away ("perfect love casts out fear," 1 John 4:18), and we can trust that He will guide us and keep us safe. When we cast our cares on Him, we can know that whatever we see in the natural is not the end of the story. He is working on our behalf. He loves the ones we love even more than we do, and we can trust Him to meet their needs and lead them to the truth.

When we know and believe the love He has for us, we won't have the trouble we once had in obeying Him when He tells us what we need to do. We will know and believe that whatever He says to do is for our benefit, and for the benefit of others around us. Mary illustrates what this looks like when Jesus performs His first miracle at the wedding of Cana.

> *On the third day there was a wedding in Cana of Galilee, and the mother of Jesus was there; and both Jesus and His disciples were invited to the wedding. When the wine ran out, the mother of Jesus said to Him, "They have no wine." And Jesus said to her, "Woman, what does that have to do with us? My hour has not yet come." His mother said to the servants, "Whatever He says to you, do it." John 2:1-5 (NASB)*

Mary trusted Jesus to do what was best in that situation for everyone involved. She was unwavering in her belief that whatever Jesus said was the right thing, and He would solve the problem at hand, however crazy it may have sounded in the natural! We can have the same rest in the midst of challenging circumstances when we trust in His wisdom and ability, not our own. We aren't smart enough to know how to navigate through life without hitting the rocks, but He is!

2. In what areas can you start trusting Him to do "far more abundantly beyond all that we ask or think" (Ephesians 3:20)?

_____

_____

Anger Toward God

What do we do when we find ourselves angry at God? Sometimes He doesn't do what we expected Him to do, when or how we expected Him to do it. The reasons can be varied, from the death of a loved one before their time, a disappointment when a miracle doesn't come when we expected it to, or the pain and damage we feel from someone we respect in the Lord hurting us. These are very real situations and produce real pain in our lives. When things happen we don't understand and don't like, we need to get back to the knowledge that God loves us and resist the temptation to draw conclusions, no matter what other people do to us or what our circumstances look like. In these situations, we need to restore our connection with our loving Heavenly Father to receive healing and wisdom from Him. He never causes evil to happen to us and has only ever sent blessing and grace upon grace to us!

> *Every good thing given and every perfect gift is from above, coming down from the Father of lights, with whom there is no variation or shifting shadow. James 1:17 (NASB)*

It is the enemy that tries to convince us that the evil in this world comes from God, and if he can convince us of this, he can cut us off from our source of help!

This is where we can use the tools we have already learned to get out of strife with God. If we need to forgive God, forgive. Not because He needs it or has made a mistake—by no means! But simply because we are in the prison of unforgiveness and we need to release God of what we, in our foolish pride, believe He owes to us. Forgiveness is a release of debt, real or imagined. Of course, we should also repent of criticism and judgment of God, because that played a part in our unforgiveness. God is so good! He will let us think He is wrong and still love us and bless us all the same, even when it was really a prison of our own making! His concern is for a restoration of the relationship!

3. Allow the Holy Spirit to reveal to you any areas you may be angry or in strife with God.

_____

_____

_____

_____

_____

4. What, if any, baits have contributed to this lack of peace with God?

_____

_____

_____

_____

_____

Take time to confess these things to God and restore your relationship with your loving Heavenly Father right now.

Peace with God's Timing in Our Lives

When we believe we know what needs to happen, it can be difficult to wait for God's timing. It is easy for us to believe that when we don't see things happening, that means nothing is happening.

> But do not let this one fact escape your notice, beloved, that with the Lord one day is like a thousand years, and a thousand years like one day. The Lord is not slow about His promise, as some count slowness, but is patient toward you, not wishing for any to perish but for all to come to repentance. 2 Peter 3:8-9 (NASB)

Every time it seems like God is being too slow, we can remember that everything He does is out of His love for us. He will wait as long as it takes, for the best possible outcome for us and for those we love. We can rest and trust that because God knows all things (1 John 3:20), He is going to do what needs to be done at the perfect time. We just need to be patient! Jesus tells a parable in Mark 4 about a farmer sowing some seed.

> *And He was saying, "The kingdom of God is like a man who casts seed upon the soil; and he goes to bed at night and gets up by day, and the seed sprouts and grows—how, he himself does not know. The soil produces crops by itself; first the blade, then the head, then the mature grain in the head. But when the crop permits, he immediately puts in the sickle, because the harvest has come." Mark 4:26-29 (NASB)*

There are a few things that a seed needs in order to germinate, grow, and mature. It needs sunlight, dirt, water, rest, and time. The seeds that have been sown in our hearts that produce righteousness (James 3:18) have the same kinds of needs in order to produce the harvest of righteousness we would like to see in our lives. We need the Light of the World, Jesus Christ, to illuminate God's Word in our lives. A personal relationship with Him ensures that the Holy Spirit is able to apply His Word to our particular situations. We need the field for the seed to grow in—our heart. We need the water of the Word to keep His seeds fresh in our heart and minds. We need peace to let the seed rest and germinate. This means staying out of strife right after church, or after we have received the Word of God for us. Remember that it is one of the ploys of the enemy to steal the word before it has a chance to take root (Matthew 13:19). Once it has germinated, the seed still takes time in order to produce a harvest of righteousness. We need to be patient!

> *My brethren, count it all joy when you fall into various trials, knowing that the testing of your faith produces patience. But let patience have its perfect work, that you may be perfect and complete, lacking nothing. James 1:2-4 (NKJV)*

We can see from this scripture that patience works in us, helping us to "be perfect and complete, lacking in nothing!" We can cooperate with God and wait patiently, or we can complain and murmur against it, but either way the seed takes time to grow. When we aren't patient, we are actually hindering the progress we want to see! Remember when the Israelites wanted to enter into the Promised Land, but were hindered for forty years because of a complaining and murmuring spirit?

When the seed of the Word of God is sown in our hearts, it will produce the fruit of holiness, but it takes our cooperation and patience to see this happen effectively.

5. Where are you resisting the timing of God in your life?

_____

_____

_____

_____

_____

Determine today to be patient with God and His timing, knowing that patience will produce a great harvest!

PEACE WITH YOURSELF

The faith which you have, have as your own conviction before God. Happy is he who does not condemn himself in what he approves. (Romans 14:22 NASB)

Because of God's forgiveness so richly lavished on us in Christ, we are now free to forgive ourselves as well. Our conscience can be satisfied knowing that our sin account was paid in full. Since we can rest in our peace with God, we can have peace with ourselves, too! In the previous chapter, we discussed peace with God and how, as we concentrate on how much God loves us, it creates the foundation for us to receive peace in that relationship. The relationship we have with ourselves is the next most important one we have, and having peace with ourselves is crucial to having a fulfilled and productive life.

Who are you to you?

This may seem like an odd question, but our relationship with ourselves can be a difficult topic to address because it requires some introspection. Many people never even contemplate their relationship with themselves, and just blindly stumble through life doing what "feels right" and hoping for the best.

From the time we are born, we are taught to judge ourselves based on the opinions of others and the pressures of popular culture. We adopt these "opinions" as our own, and heap judgements and criticisms upon ourselves because "if those people believe I am that way, I must be that way."

The mirror is an iconic visual in regard to self-examination. When you look in the mirror, do you see someone you like? Do you see someone Jesus died for and who is deeply loved, or do you see someone who doesn't measure up or isn't performing well enough? Do you ever hear these things in your head?

"Why did I do that?!"

"I'm such an idiot!"

"I wish I were as funny as…"

"I wish I were thinner."

"I wish I were in better shape."

"God can't use me to…"

"I'll never fulfill God's plans for me."

"If I could just quit doing… I'd be so much happier!"

1. What is your opinion about yourself? List some adjectives to describe yourself.

_____

_____

_____

_____

Give Yourself a Break!

The baits can be used against ourselves as well as others and God. We can criticize, judge, or worry over ourselves, and be unwilling to forgive ourselves. Whenever we "take the bait" in any of these areas, we are out of God's peace. God wants us to walk in love with ourselves because we can only love others to the extent that we love ourselves (Matthew 22:39). We all make mistakes. If we are critical of ourselves, we end up being critical of others. What we practice on ourselves, whether it's love or judgment, is what we perform on others.

We can't judge ourselves correctly anyway! We don't always know why we do what we do. Sometimes we do things because that's the way we have seen it done, or that's the way someone treated us in the past and it just comes out of us. We need to give ourselves a break and choose to move forward with God despite our imperfections.

Even though Paul was an apostle and extremely knowledgeable about the law, even he didn't judge himself. He knew that he was going to get more progress out of forgiving himself and abiding in God, than he ever was by criticizing and judging his own thoughts and behavior.

> *But to me it is a very small thing that I may be examined by you, or by any human court; in fact, I do not even examine myself. For I am conscious of nothing against myself, yet I am not by this acquitted; but the one who examines me is the Lord. Therefore do not go on passing judgment before the time, but wait until the Lord comes who will both bring to light the things hidden in the darkness and disclose the motives of men's hearts; and then each man's praise will come to him from God. 1 Corinthians 4:3-5 (NASB)*

Notice he said "praise" in verse 5 and not "praise and judgment." Jesus was already judged and punished for our iniquities (Isaiah 53:5), which are the evil desires, weaknesses, and sins in our hearts. Jesus said in John 5:24,

> *Most assuredly, I say to you, he who hears My word and believes in Him who sent Me has everlasting life, and shall not come into judgment, but has passed from death into life. (NKJV)*

Because Jesus took all our judgment on the cross, we get all His everlasting life! We have passed out of death, condemnation, and judgment, and into His abundant life. Hallelujah!

2. What are some situations in your life where you need to give yourself a break?

_____

_____

_____

_____

To be clear, when we advocate giving ourselves a break, we are not meaning for you to take sin lightly. Willful disobedience takes us out of submission to God, out of peace, and thus out of God's best for our lives. Remember, the mind set on the flesh—which is where rebellion comes from—is death! The act of giving ourselves a break is to resist the condemnation that can come when we miss it in our relationship with God. If we will give ourselves a break—forgive ourselves—we can see clearly and begin to function in the knowledge of the mercy and grace of God. This allows us to move forward in our lives and grow. We cannot give ourselves a break over a sin of which we are unrepentant. We need to go back and truly repent over this sin first, submit ourselves before God, resist the enemy, and then we can give ourselves a break, remembering that Jesus has paid for every bit of every sin in our lives through His sacrifice.

See Yourself in Christ

We learned earlier that the real "us" is our new, recreated spirit. When we were born again, we became a new creature in Christ, a new "mini-Jesus!" When we start to agree with who God says we are in Christ, we are going to like ourselves much, much more! Instead of looking to our behavior or our past to determine who we are and what we are like, we can look to His Word and believe what He says we are as a new creature in Christ Jesus! Here are some faith-building facts about our new identities.

God is working in our lives.

For we are His workmanship, created in Christ Jesus for good works, which God prepared beforehand so that we would walk in them. Ephesians 2:10 (NASB)

We are righteous in Jesus.

He made Him who knew no sin to be sin on our behalf, so that we might become the righteousness of God in Him. 2 Corinthians 5:21 (NASB)

We have the mind of Christ.

For who has known or understood the mind (the counsels and purposes) of the Lord so as to guide and instruct Him and give Him knowledge? But we have the mind of Christ (the Messiah) and do hold the thoughts (feelings and purposes) of His heart. 1 Corinthians 2:16 (AMP)

Going to God's Word and finding out who we are "in Him" or "in Christ" is going to free us from the chains of our past and help us to walk in all we have been given in Christ. Hebrews 12:1-2 tells us to

Lay aside every encumbrance and the sin which so easily entangles us, and let us run with endurance the race that is set before us, fixing our eyes on Jesus, the author and perfecter of faith, who for the joy set before Him endured the cross, despising the shame, and has sat down at the right hand of the throne of God. (NASB)

Paul says he forgets his past, and only looks toward Jesus as his goal and example to follow.

Brethren, I do not regard myself as having laid hold of it yet; but one thing I do: forgetting what lies behind and reaching forward to what lies ahead, I press on toward the goal for the prize of the upward call of God in Christ Jesus.
Philippians 3:13-14 (NASB)

We can't "forget what lies behind" and "run with endurance the race that is set before us" with unforgiveness toward ourselves in our hearts. This is a bait, and we have to repent of it and forgive ourselves, whatever we have done. Jesus has paid a heavy price for that forgiveness, and by not receiving it, we are essentially telling God that Jesus's death was not enough. Since God says Jesus's sacrifice was more than enough to cover all our debts with God, who are we to say it isn't? It is a command of God for us to forgive others and ourselves, even as God forgave us in Christ.

If we find regrets in our hearts over things in our past, these can be a red flag signaling that we are still in condemnation or unforgiveness with ourselves. We need to confess our sins, ask for God's forgiveness and the forgiveness of others if possible, forgive ourselves, and forget our past by looking to Jesus as our righteousness, knowing He paid for all of our sins. When we are free of regrets, we are able to love God, ourselves, and others freely, and walk in a greater level of the peace of God.

Satan may also bring to our remembrance things we have done in the past—things we did wrong or regret doing. While it is true that those things happened, it is also true that we are forgiven and that our sins are removed from us as far as the east is from the west (Psalm 103:12). We can stand up on the inside and tell the devil,

"It's true I did that, but I'm forgiven and it's all gone!" We can't let it dwell in our minds and get our emotions all stirred up. We remind the devil that we are forgiven by God, we've forgiven ourselves, and it doesn't exist anymore. This is a powerful action and will set us free from the torment of regret that the enemy tries to put on us.

Confessing God's Word over our lives is a great exercise to build our faith and orientate our mind and emotions to be in line with the truth.

Look up the following scriptures and rewrite them using first person so that you can confess over yourselves what the Word of God says about you.

1 John 3:3   1 John 4:13

1 John 5:14-15   John 15:7-11

Ephesians 1:4a

Let God Be in Charge of Our Growth

Sometimes we believe our spiritual growth is completely our own responsibility and we carry the weight of our perceived spiritual maturity on our own shoulders. We can become frustrated when we don't seem to be maturing as soon as we would like, or if we continue to struggle with the same issues. Only God really knows how long it will take for us to really be able to incorporate new revelation into our lives. We need to just give ourselves a break, and let God be in charge of our spiritual growth. We cannot accurately judge how well we are doing anyway!

Jesus is the "author and perfecter of our faith," and is very capable of reproving us when we are in error, and gently leading us into His glorious truth. We need to trust God to know what we need to work on, and cooperate with Him. We can trust Him to change us and teach us. He can get right to the heart of any issues we have and cut us free from the root cause, cutting off the bad fruit we are bearing as well.

Here are some helpful confessions to speak over your life to get your thinking in line with the Word of God regarding His leadership over your life.

I hear His voice and follow Him.

> *My sheep hear My voice, and I know them, and they follow Me.*
> *John 10:27 (NASB)*

I am led by the Spirit of God.

> *For all who are being led by the Spirit of God, these are sons of God. Romans 8:14 (NASB)*

I trust in the Lord, and He directs my path.

> *Trust in the Lord with all your heart and do not lean on your own understanding. In all your ways acknowledge Him, and He will make your paths straight. Proverbs 3:5-6 (NASB)*

Commit to trusting God with your spiritual growth, and not judging or criticizing yourself because of your faults.

3. List some areas of your life you would like to see changed and commit them to the Lord.

_____

_____

_____

_____

_____

Benefits of Being at Peace with Ourselves

We can just "be" ourselves when we might otherwise have been chasing or running away from unresolved issues. When we are at peace with ourselves, we can wake up in the morning and just enjoy our days instead of carrying around rejections, disappointments, or other baggage in addition to trying to live our lives.

Being at peace with ourselves is so important. We have to deal with so much in life without our own internal struggles making it worse. One of the main principles of walking in powerful peace is to break out of the chains that bind us as we find them. This enables us to have the freedom that Christ came to bring us.

> *It is for freedom that Christ has set us free. Stand firm, then, and do not let yourselves be burdened again by a yoke of slavery. Galatians 5:1 (NIV)*

Peace with ourselves comes from knowing we are loved, not based on what we do, but on who God says we are in Him. If our self-worth is based on who God says we are and His love for us, then everything else is no big deal.

It is important for us to love ourselves because the Bible says, "You shall love your neighbor as yourself" (Matthew 22:39), so if we don't love ourselves, we are not going to love to other people. John says, "We love, because He first loved us" (1 John 4:19). When we receive His love for us, we can then love ourselves and are able, out of our abundance, to love others. We are able to minister to others out of our abundance, but not out of our lack (Matthew 10:8).

When we have a great relationship with God, and love ourselves, we have laid the foundation to having peace with everyone else.

> *If possible, so far as it depends on you, be at peace with all men.*
> *Romans 12:18 (KJV)*

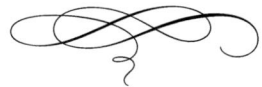

Chapter Twenty

PEACE WITH YOUR SPOUSE

Sharon and I were married in August of 1992. We were both young, in love, loved Jesus, and knew nothing about what we had really signed up for relating to being a good spouse. We were young in the Lord and ignorant of how to walk in peace with each other. The biggest asset we each had was an overall desire to serve God, and that was all He needed to perform His miracles. There were many times we believed our marriage was over but as we learned to submit to God and stay away from the baits, God kept us together and we are more in love now than ever. This chapter is a greatest-hits of the principles and values we have learned from God on how to walk in peace with each other. —Greg

A Peaceful Marriage

Thousands of people every year head off into a marriage without the skills needed to keep it together. Couple that with the possibility that neither person was raised in a peaceful home, where they saw these principles displayed, and we can see why the divorce rate is so high these days.

We know that God hates divorce (Malachi 2:16), but we may not have ever thought about why this is. We can get insight into this by looking at John 3:16.

> *For God so loved the world that he gave his one and only Son, that whoever believes in him shall not perish but have eternal life. (NIV)*

God loved the world so much that He did what it took to restore the relationship. This is a marvelous example for us all, especially in marriage. So one reason God hates divorce is because He is all about relationships and restoring ones that are in trouble. He also is faithful to do His part and will never give up on us. Hallelujah! This characteristic is one we should ascribe to in the marriage relationship if possible. It isn't always possible, but should be our general attitude and goal within a normal marriage situation. Doing this puts us in the best possible mindset for God to work with us, and limits the ammunition the enemy sends our way to distract us.

1. What would you like your marriage to look like? What are some characteristics you would like to see expressed on a daily basis?

_____

_____

_____

_____

_____

_____

Benefits of a Peaceful Marriage

By this time, we have a pretty good idea of the benefits of peace, but now we will discuss some of the specific benefits of a peaceful marriage.

Prayer of agreement

There are going to be many obstacles and challenges that comes for those who get married, and we will need each other as a support partner for those times. The prayer of agreement (Matthew 18:19) is an amazing gift to married believers. We have seen God do some amazing things in our lives based on the prayer of agreement and walking in unity. Satan would love for us to be in such division that we never have the opportunity to agree with one another in prayer. He wants to keep us in strife and be ineffective. The prayer of agreement focuses us on goals that we are believing God for, and helps us resist the enemy's plans to tear us down.

Peace in the home and with the children

When God first approached me about getting the strife out of my marriage, He used my children as leverage. I wasn't willing to make the changes necessary in myself just for Greg. When we first started studying peace, I could barely be in the same room with him without glaring! However, God knew I would do anything for my children to grow up into be all that He wanted them to be. He showed me that if we would walk in peace and resist strife in our home, my children would be spared the rebellion and confusion mentioned in James 3:16. It was worth it to me to endure whatever He needed to change in me in order for my kids to fulfill His perfect plans for them! I have since developed a deep love for my husband, and I can say with certainty that as you learn to walk in peace with your spouse, you will begin to enjoy heaven on earth in your marriage! It is truly a wonderful blessing! —Sharon

When there is an atmosphere of peace between spouses, it is transferred to the rest of the home. When parents are giving each other a break, the kids will be more loving as well.

> *And knowing their thoughts Jesus said to them, "Any kingdom divided against itself is laid waste; and any city or house divided against itself will not stand." Matthew 12:25 (NASB)*

So we can deduce from this that a house that is not divided WILL stand! Hallelujah! When we are training our children to walk in peace and love by our example, they will walk in peace and love as well, and continue to do so as they become victorious adults!

> *Train up a child in the way he should go, Even when he is old he will not depart from it. Proverbs 22:6 (NASB)*

Trust

Trust between husband and wife is a natural by-product of walking in peace and love. When a husband knows his wife isn't criticizing him and judging the things he does, he will naturally let down his guard and trust her with his intimate secrets. When a wife knows her husband loves her and forgives her unconditionally, she will relax around him and be herself with him as well. The goals of the husband and wife are also accomplished because they aren't spinning their wheels in arguing and strife. We have discussed the wonderful power that comes with unity in a previous chapter. This power is released in the marriage relationship as well, when a husband and wife determine to walk in peace and walk in submission to God's will for them and their family.

2. Which of these areas is a challenge for you in your marriage? Give it some honest thought.

_____

_____

_____

_____

_____

Who Does What?

There are as many opinions about who is supposed to do what in a marriage as there are marriages! What should our opinions be, based on the Word of God?

Our spouse is unique and valuable (Psalm 139:14). We cannot reproduce the value of our spouse no matter how hard we try—it will always be different. We need to learn to value the difference or *different-ness* of our spouse, and learn why God put us together with them in the first place (Ephesians 2:10).

Women: some people says that women don't need a husband. Some say men are weak, stupid, untrustworthy, insensitive, and inferior to women All these lies steal a good husband from you in all practicality. Men: the same goes for you who believe your wives are inferior, and should be subservient. Believing these lies just steals a good wife from you and your reality. We need to purposefully shun popular culture when it concerns who our spouses are, and instead find what God's word says about them and believe that. We get to enjoy an amazing gift to us from God in our spouse, but if we are reacting to each other out of strife, we will miss this blessing.

God created the earth and all of its intertwined complexity so that species derive mutual benefit from one another. God has done the same thing as it pertains to the relationship of husband and wife. When a couple is operating in their God-given capacities, whatever that may be, they are going to be fulfilled and successful, and life will be much easier. That doesn't mean that the husband's role is always to keep the family finances and mow the yard, or that the wife's role is to cook and stay home with the children. Each family is unique and God has gifted every member with unique gifts to use to bless the rest of the family. God has anointed the husband to be the loving head of the wife positionally and lead the family (Ephesians 5:22-24), and the wife is anointed to respectfully give Godly counsel to her husband (Proverbs 31:11). These are only positions of authority and structure for the purpose of order, and are not meant to imply importance or superiority or inferiority at all.

If we look at what Paul taught the Corinthian church in 1 Corinthians 12:12-18, we see that God places us where He wants us and gifts us to fulfill His purposes for us accordingly.

> For even as the body is one and yet has many members, and all the members of the body, though they are many, are one body, so also is Christ. For by one Spirit we were all baptized into one body, whether Jews or Greeks, whether slaves or free, and we were all made to drink of one Spirit. For the body is not one member, but many. If the foot says, "Because I am not a hand, I am not a part of the body," it is not for this reason any the less a part of the body. And if the ear says, "Because I am not an eye, I am not a part of the body," it is not for this reason any the less a part of the body. If the whole body were an eye, where would the hearing be? If the whole were hearing, where would the sense of smell be? But now God has placed the members, each one of them, in the body, just as He desired. 1 Corinthians 12:12-18 (NASB)

We are all under Christ's authority and there is no one superior or inferior to another. There are just different positions in the family company to help facilitate order and function!

A marriage is going to be happy and blessed when there is unity of purpose, and everyone is working toward the common goals using their unique gifts according to their calling.

3. Who has shaped your ideas about the different roles in marriage?

_____

_____

_____

_____

_____

_____

4. Where do you need to revise your ideas about marriage according to God's Word?

_____

_____

_____

_____

_____

Washing Our Brain

Everyday, our enemy is trying to "brain-wash" us into thinking thoughts that will produce death in our lives or the lives of others. He uses television, our friends, and anyone we listen to in order to try and sow seeds into our hearts that will disagree with what God says and wants for us. He has been doing this for years and the mental strongholds of lies in our minds concerning our spouse and marriage have to be revealed and eliminated in order for us to have powerful peace in our homes.

If we want to change what we are thinking about our spouse, and "wash" our belief system from old carnal thinking, we need to repeatedly expose our thinking to the Word of God. "Brain-washing" is used in a negative sense in the secular world to get people to believe whatever ideas that a cult, authority figure, or even a corporation wants their followers, constituents, or consumers to believe. By exposing someone to a fact over and over and over again, we can eventually change what they believe whether it is good or bad, true or false.

An example of this happened in my life not too long ago. I noticed I had been harboring some negative emotions toward my husband and it was hard to trust him and enjoy spending time with him. I prayed about this, because that's no way to enjoy your marriage, and the Lord showed me where I had been believing some lies about Greg. Mainly that he didn't really love me, and that when he apologized for something he said that had hurt my feelings, he hadn't really meant it. As I chose those judgmental thoughts over forgiveness and believing the best, my emotions had followed suit and had grown negative. As I repented and confessed my error to Greg, he forgave me and our fellowship was restored and our marriage was joyful once again! —Sharon

We can literally change our thinking to be in line with the truth by speaking God's Word repeatedly to ourselves, submitting to it, and imagining it to be true until we replace the old thinking with the new.

So faith comes from hearing, and hearing by the word of Christ. Romans 10:17 (NASB)

What we need to understand is that our enemy has been doing this for years! In how many sitcoms is the wife a controlling nag and the husband an idiot? Almost every show teaches people how to insult and demean their spouse and wraps it in the veil of humor. This is not God's best for our marriages and will only hurt our spouses.

Let no foul or polluting language, nor evil word nor unwholesome or worthless talk [ever] come out of your mouth, but only such [speech] as is good and beneficial to the spiritual progress of others, as is fitting to the need and the occasion, that it may be a blessing and give grace (God's favor) to those who hear it. Ephesians 4:29 (AMP)

Of course we can still watch sitcoms and enjoy the shows we like to watch, but that thinking can seep into our belief system if it remains unchallenged by the Word of God. Also, we can't get into a habit of insulting each other under the guise of just trying to be funny. We might think it is harmless, but humor can be based on truth, and this kind of behavior damages real people and destroys trust. The really cool thing is we can allow the Holy Spirit to use God's Word to illuminate what is really going on in our hearts.

For the word of God is alive and powerful. It is sharper than the sharpest two-edged sword, cutting between soul and spirit, between joint and marrow. It exposes our innermost thoughts and desires. Hebrews 4:12 (NLT)

We need to be mindful of the long-term effects "coarse jesting" can have on the people we love most. Are the words we are saying blessing them? Are our words giving them grace that will help them be a better person/spouse/parent? We need to "wash" or renew our minds to understand that such behavior toward our spouse doesn't help us achieve God's best for our lives. We can then ask God to help us speak words that build others up and help us move forward in His perfect will.

As we abide in Him, He will lead us to change our habits that are producing rotten fruit in our marriages. To replace the negative beliefs we are holding doesn't take long, it just takes serious submission to God to meditate on His Word regularly. Here is an example... Instead of exposing ourselves to a worldly sitcom for half an hour, we can trade that time in for 30 minutes in the Word, finding out what God says about our spouses, and saying that instead. Here are some great starting scriptures for our study.

Marriage

Ephesians 4:31,32	Ephesians 4:23,24	Ephesians 5:1,2
2 Timothy 2:26	Matthew 18:18	

Husbands

Matthew 18:18	Ephesians 5:22,23	Genesis 2:18
1 Corinthians 7:3-5	Proverbs 18:22	1 Peter 3:7-9
Proverbs 3:3,4	Psalm 112:1-4	Proverbs 31:28-31

Wives

Proverbs 19:14	1 Peter 3:1-9	Ephesians 5:22,33
1 Cor. 7:2-5	Proverbs 31:25-27	Proverbs 12:4
Proverbs 14:1		

When we begin believing our spouse is who the Word says they are, and that they do what the Word says they do, we are going to find it really hard to not like them! It's amazing how easy it is as we submit to God and walk in the spirit and love!

The devil already understands the power of what we believe about each other. He wants us to believe our spouse wants to control us, or that our spouse doesn't love us, or that our spouse is being selfish. When we are doing this, everything our spouse does is colored by this deception. Everything our spouse says sounds like something else to us. We are deceived by a lie and in bondage to it. We need the truth of God's Word to set us free so we can enjoy the marriage God has given us! The marriage we already have is probably ten times better than we think it is, but we are just deceived by the lies we've been told... that it is much worse!

Being mindful of the baits can help us in a practical way in this. When we find we are in strife with our spouse, we can trace back our conversation or thinking until we find where we have been critical, judgmental, or unforgiving and REPENT! We need to ask for forgiveness from our spouse if it will build bridges between us and restore the relationship. It is not worth being out of God's peace for a second to hold on to those corrosive behaviors!

> *Therefore, since we are surrounded by such a huge crowd of witnesses to the life of faith, let us strip off every weight that slows us down, especially the sin that so easily trips us up. And let us run with endurance the race God has set before us. Hebrews 12:1 (NLT)*

Now, if we have just been critical or judgmental or unforgiving in our heart and our spouse has no idea, we might just need to confess this to God and repent in our heart. We need to be led by the Spirit of God and He will show us how to restore things. If we have been harboring lies about our spouse, it may do damage to them to hear what the lies are, so we need to be sure whatever we do is out of love and for their benefit and edification. God knows what would be best, so ask Him and obey!

After we discover what we have been erroneously believing, we need to replace these thoughts with what God says. This is the difference between the mind set on the flesh in our marriage and the mind set on the spirit. If we were believing that our connection to the Holy Spirit is better than our spouse's—which is pride—we could start proclaiming "My sheep hear my voice..." and believing it about our spouse— which is believing the best instead. Sometimes the believing takes time, and that's okay. We can just keep doing the"washing of water with the word" (Ephesians 5:26) on our thinking. We will find our opinion about our spouse begins to change as we quit believing the worst and start believing the best about our spouse!

The awesome thing about God's Word, when we choose to apply it to our lives and our situations by faith, is that it actually changes what is going on in the natural to be in agreement with God's will. The ideas about our spouse from sitcoms, our parents, or our friends are no match for the power found in God's Word. God's Word created the heavens and the earth out of nothing! It can rebuild us from the inside out and change any situation if we will submit to it and use it! We will start to have the marriage we want and it will be heaven on earth!

Of course our spouse still has free will. If they choose to rebel against what God wants in their life, God will let them. Either way, the best thing we can do is to pray for them. Praying and believing the best over them, however, will ensure that we are doing nothing to hinder the work of the Holy Spirit in their life as they grow, and God is free to work on our behalf in their heart. And as we genuinely believe the best, the love of God will flow through us to them, and God's love never fails!

5. What are some lies you might have been believing about who your spouse is, or why they are doing what they are doing?

_____

_____

_____

_____

_____

_____

6. What does God's Word say about those things?

_____

_____

_____

_____

_____

_____

Having the Marriage We Want

At some point in our marriage we have to decide what is most important to us: handling every offense as it comes along, or staying in peace and power by choosing to walk in forgiveness and not being easily offended. It is actually possible for a married couple to disagree and not talk it out, but allow God to move and set things right. We've heard there are three sides to every story: my side, your side, and the truth! Only God knows what's really going on, and as we choose peace and righteousness over being right, we will see Him become our Defender and Lover of our souls and gently lead us and our spouse to the truth.

Here is a great exercise the next time we are having trouble communicating with our spouses and seem to be arguing more than getting along. Sometimes we just can't dig out of an emotional hole; we just have to declare the end of hostilities and hit reset. When this occurs, we can make ourselves hold hands with our spouse, look each other in the eyes and say, "Let's just have the marriage we want!" Marriage works best if we can both be more focused on having the marriage we want instead of solving every little disagreement at hand.

What do we do if we don't agree?

We don't have to have an argument, we can just choose to disagree. Every disagreement doesn't need to be resolved. We can choose to just give it over to God and choose peace in the home and let God have control. This will require us to totally let go and release our spouse in order for God to be able to move and give us His best. It's foolish to believe that we have to work out the problem RIGHT NOW. We can move on and live our lives in peace even with unsettled situations around us. We can be happy, make up, have fun, go to a movie, go to dinner, go for a walk and hold hands all while professing our love for each other. We can let God be in charge of that contentious situation as we choose to not have an opinion. This is a great exercise in choosing what is truly important at that very moment, giving up what we want, and prioritizing God's peace and blessing on us and our home. This is "self-control," which is a fruit of the spirit. The enemy will drive us to settle it at all costs. The devil would have us believe that what we are fighting for is SO important that it is worth throwing away our peace to get it resolved RIGHT NOW. That is a lie that will rob us of God's presence and peace that we desperately need if we are going to walk in victory in any situation. Obviously, if the house is on fire or the situation doesn't lend itself to talking it out, we can't sit there and argue about whose fault it is. We can figure all that out later. The most important thing is to prioritize the union of our marriage and the peace of God which we all need so badly. In the day to day "working things out" life, God wants to be the umpire between us and our spouse as we submit our wills to Him and walk in the spirit.

Let the peace (soul harmony which comes) from Christ rule (act as umpire continually) in your hearts [deciding and settling with finality all questions that arise in your minds, in that peaceful state] to which as [members of Christ's] one body you were also called [to live]. And be thankful (appreciative), [giving praise to God always].
Colossians 3:15 (AMP)

God cares about our situation, but we need to realize He might start by working on us first. He will most likely work on our spouse as well, but many times it will start with us. Quite often, He wants us to not be dependent on our spouse changing, so He will work on us until we no longer care if the other person changes or not and then He will work on them. This is because He wants us to be free. Galatians 5:1 tells us, "It is for freedom that Christ has set us free." This is one of God's main motives, that His people be free. How are we to be free? We are free when we aren't concerned about what our spouse does or doesn't do or say, and we want what God wants for us, which is peace. This freedom really burns the devil up when he can't use our marriage as a punching bag to get at us because we won't take the baits or walk in the flesh.

What if my spouse isn't a Christian?

Paul gives specific instructions for the saved man or woman married to a non-Christian in 1 Corinthians 7:12-16.

But to the rest I say, not the Lord, that if any brother has a wife who is an unbeliever, and she consents to live with him, he must not divorce her. And a woman who has an unbelieving husband, and he consents to live with her, she must not send her husband away. For the unbelieving husband is sanctified through his wife, and the unbelieving wife is sanctified through her believing husband; for otherwise your children are unclean, but now they are holy. Yet if the unbelieving one leaves, let him leave; the brother or the sister is not under bondage in such cases, but God has called us to peace. For how do you know, O wife, whether you will save your husband? Or how do you know, O husband, whether you will save your wife? (NASB)

When we are walking in peace, the Holy Spirit is able to move on our behalf and minister to our unsaved spouse and our children. Our children are set apart for God's purposes as well. We, as Christians, also have a great deal of authority over the devil in our own homes and can rebuke him away from our family. Finally, we can commit to walking in love and peace with this person, which also includes "living it" instead of only "preaching it"—showing them the love of Jesus in action, walking in the peace of Christ in our daily living, asking for forgiveness from them when we mess up, praying for their benefit and for God to bless them. Don't know what to pray? Pray Ephesians 3:16-19 over them.

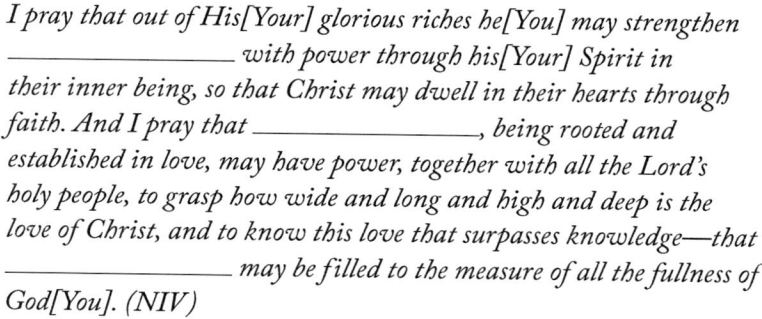

I pray that out of His[Your] glorious riches he[You] may strengthen _____ with power through his[Your] Spirit in their inner being, so that Christ may dwell in their hearts through faith. And I pray that _____, being rooted and established in love, may have power, together with all the Lord's holy people, to grasp how wide and long and high and deep is the love of Christ, and to know this love that surpasses knowledge—that _____ may be filled to the measure of all the fullness of God[You]. (NIV)

What a marvelous gift to go before our Heavenly Father on behalf of our spouse and intercede for them. This is the love of Jesus in action, and God will move on this act of faith as we stay in peace.

What if my spouse is violent?

Violence in marriage and home life cannot be tolerated. If you are in a violent situation, please get out and seek help!

What about the Christian spouse not submitted to God's Word?

We all fail from time and time and get out of God's will for our lives and end up walking in the flesh. When this happens, we get to pray for one another and encourage one another in the Word of God. As the husband or wife continues on with the Lord and follows Him, the disobedient spouse will be pricked with conviction. By walking in love, patience, and forgiveness, we are blessing our spouse and staying in peace ourselves. When we do this, God moves on our behalf!

In the same way, you wives, be submissive to your own husbands so that even if any of them are disobedient to the word, they may be won without a word by the behavior of their wives, as they observe your chaste and respectful behavior.
1 Peter 3:1-2 (NASB)

When wives are submitting to their husbands, they are in a very powerful position. They are cooperating with the Holy Spirit in getting the attention of their husbands if they are in error somewhere. If a wife will choose to trust God when hubby gets it wrong, God will bless any situation! We all get it wrong from time to time—we must give our spouse a break. God can cause anything to turn around for good in our lives if we let Him!

We are not saying any of us should ever break the law or disobey God's command because of our spouse. Obviously that would be a bad idea! In all these situations, God is calling us to a life of peace. There won't be peace for the married couple if one or both of them are arrested and sent to prison for crime!

Can I marry a non-Christian so that they might get saved?

If you are a single Christian, you should only marry a Christian. Paul tells us in 2 Corinthians,

Do not be bound together with unbelievers; for what partnership have righteousness and lawlessness, or what fellowship has light with darkness? - 2 Corinthians 6:14 (NASB)

Unity in spirit is very important before we seek to be bound for life in marriage to someone. A non-Christian is in the state we were before Christ and under the headship of the enemy until such time as he or she becomes a Christian. A Christian and non-Christian don't have the same goals, aren't going the same direction, and will live life completely different in very serious ways. A Christian cannot have a real partnership and fellowship with a non-Christian. God's purpose for marriage was to give us a living earthly example of Christ and the church (Ephesians 5:21-32). This can't happen if the representatives of "Christ" or the "church" in this scenario aren't actually submitted to Christ! God is trying to save the Christian from what might be years of pain and sorrow. The Christian spouse would always be seeking to please God, and the non-Christian spouse would be seeking to please him or herself.

God's Value System

Many conflicts in marriage come from incompatibility between value systems. What does this mean? This is when the things that the husband and wife value don't line up and they end up disagreeing on which way to go. An example could be that the husband wants to spend some extra money on a shed in the backyard while the wife wants to redecorate the kitchen. While this may seem trivial, these little things are the areas in which the enemy spends a great amount of time trying to establish strife.

Let's perform a little experiment between you and your spouse. On a piece of paper, put these 10 items in order of importance from 1-10, with 1 being the most important and 10 being the least.

Money	Parenting	Spouse	Vacation	Church
Respect	In-laws	Housework	Sex	Peace in home

1. _____   6. _____

2. _____   7. _____

3. _____   8. _____

4. _____   9. _____

5. _____   10. _____

After you have completed your list, lay it down next to your spouse's list and compare. Be careful not to question or criticize each other's choices at this time— we don't want to get into strife.

Most likely, there will be some differences in our lists, and possibly some dramatic ones. This is an example of the value system incongruences we are talking about. Sometimes these can lead to disagreements that can charge a relationship with strife.

Can two walk together, except they be agreed? (Amos 3:3 KJV)

While it is unlikely to agree on everything, the main point isn't that we actually agree on the order of every topic, but rather that we correctly choose to act in a way that agrees with our agreed-upon priorities. i.e. -- Is this situation worth my/our peace? Is this worth having an argument over. or can I/we just trust God with it? Too many times we elevate our own desires and push our will onto the other person because we believe our way is the best way or even God's way. When we compromise the peace in our home, we have lost—even if we win. At that point we become a sucker for the enemy and will have a messy relationship to clean up.

The interesting thing about this experiment is that the right answers will change with the specifics of the immediate situation. The key is to become more aware of the choices we make on a daily basis, and how we as husbands and wives can work together on those choices and prioritize peace in our marriages and homes. God has promised to help us figure out these value decisions as we walk in the spirit.

> *But if any of you lacks wisdom, let him ask of God, who gives to all generously and without reproach, and it will be given to him.*
> *James 1:5 (NASB)*

So, when we are at an impasse with our spouse and can sense a conflict brewing, we need to be careful with our words and listen for God to speak to us and define His value system. We can consult His Word about the topic, and we need to be willing to release our desires to His will. Many times we have been passionate about a topic and God will give us pause and tell us that it's not worth it. We have to just drop it and not talk about it or give up what we want because we are more in love with what He wants. It is always worth the price we pay.

Jesus encountered this very thing when He was in the garden praying the night before His death. It was His weakest moment and He could have blown it all. The devil was working overtime on Him and He cried out to God "If there be any other way!" but caught Himself and quickly put Himself last and exalted God's best in that situation. It was a real moment of decision for Him. The Bible says in Hebrews 4:15,

> *For we do not have a high priest who is unable to sympathize with our weaknesses, but we have one who has been tempted in every way, just as we are--yet was without sin. (NIV)*

Jesus knows what we go through, and our Heavenly Father's grace is sufficient (2 Corinthians 12:9) for us when we need it. We have to choose God's way over our own way, realizing that doing so causes the crucifixion of the flesh and will bring amazing fruit in the spirit. God knows we have choices and is pleased when we choose His way instead of our own. This is faith, plain and simple, and it causes God to move.

Words of Wisdom

We do not consider ourselves the experts on marriage. but we do feel that we have a good marriage. We would like to share some of the nuggets of wisdom we have acquired over the decades we have been together.

"I am not responsible for what you don't tell me."

This was one of the first lessons we learned and we still use it today! It is simply about good communication. Too many times we hold others responsible for our unmet, unvocalized expectations.

"I think I'm right, but I may be wrong."

An argument-ender that Joyce Meyer mentions in her book *Life Without Strife* is to simply say, "I think I'm right, but I may be wrong." This allows us to state our beliefs, but also allows that we might not have all the facts and/or our reasoning might be flawed. This also helps us to stay in humility, because we are ALL wrong at times!

It's more important to be righteous, than to be right.

It is better to keep our influence and God's blessings than to get our way. If we push our will or opinion on our spouse, it will lead to resentment and subsequent loss of peace. We will also lose our influence with that person. This takes us out of the game, so to speak, and we can't make a difference if we are not in the game (this goes for all relationships, not just marriages).

Invisible shoeboxes

There are times when a minor disagreement or discussion suddenly turns major in what seems like a matter of seconds. A floodgate of negative emotions is inundating the situation from one or both spouses over what is, in reality, a very minor issue. We have found that something has tripped open an "invisible shoebox" of serious issues that had never been dealt with before, or had been dealt with incompletely. We have all had serious disappointments, rejections, or other negative circumstances in our lives. How we have dealt with these will determine if we can move on in freedom or not. If we try to ignore our pains and sorrows and refuse to deal with them, they don't really go away. It is sort of like having an invisible shoebox stuffed full of emotional baggage from an undealt-with situation hidden under our bed. When someone else comes along, they can accidentally kick it open when they do something to remind us of these issues, and spill its contents onto the floor in front of us. Suddenly we are both dealing with a level 10 response to what should have been maybe a level 2 or 3 problem.

If we find ourselves with a kicked open "invisible shoebox" or two, we need to remember that our spouse is not our enemy and only wants to help us. We need to remember that God is with us and can bless us with wisdom as we go through painful issues, and lead us to the truth that will set us free. Many times, these issues are so emotionally charged it is difficult to see clearly what is going on. Some time alone in prayer can help us to reset and get God's perspective. We needn't be afraid to apologize for hurting our spouse during these times. Reconciliation can begin with a heartfelt, "I'm sorry." We can remember,

> *And we know that in all things God works for the good of those who love him, who have been called according to his purpose. Romans 8:28 (NIV)*

The pain we go through now can lead to blessing later. God may even use us to minister to others that have suffered similar life experiences. It is immensely satisfying to be able to help others through the things we have conquered by God's grace!

Don't make it worse.

When we find ourselves in a heated "discussion" with our spouse, sometimes the best course of action is to STOP TALKING!

> *When there are many words, transgression is unavoidable, but he who restrains his lips is wise. Proverbs 10:19 (NASB).*

We can remember what our mothers taught us, "If you can't say anything nice, don't say anything at all." Many times, when words cease, the emotions that have been churning inside start to die down and a calm comes. If an issue is real and needs to be addressed, it can be done in a calm, patient, and respectful way as each person is seeking first to understand and then to be understood.

Having God's Best for our lives means we are willing to pay the price for God to have His will done. Wanting God's best for our life, our spouse, our home life, and our kids will motivate us to push past hurt feelings, arguments, hopelessness, and anger. It can be a great motivator. If we have His best in our lives, the fruit we will be bearing will be amazing, and it will affect the lives of everyone around us.

It will be everything we actually wanted in our hearts. What would have happened to Adam and Eve if they had asked themselves before they ate the forbidden fruit, "Is this God's best for us?"

God has placed us together with our spouse for a reason, and the perspective our spouse holds is SUPPOSED to be different than ours. If we were both exactly the same, one of us would be unnecessary. When we can learn to enjoy and appreciate the differences in our spouse, our marriage is on the way to heaven on earth!

7. Set a time this week to meditate on your value system. Let God speak to you about His value system and yield to it as He reveals His priorities for your life. Write down what you believe God thinks is most important in your life and what He wants you to do about it.

_____

_____

_____

_____

_____

For the Wives:

There are few things the Lord has shown us during our years of marriage that might be of some help as we seek to hold our peace in our marital bliss!

Pray before you bring an opinion or word of wisdom to your husband about a major issue. This will help your counsel to be Godly and right. If they take it, great! If not, pray some more, and trust God to work it all out for your benefit (Rom. 8:28, 1 Peter 3:1).

Don't try and be the Holy Spirit for your husband. John 16:8 says, "When he comes, he will convict the world of guilt in regard to sin and righteousness and judgment" (NIV-1984). We can try and be the Holy Spirit for our husbands, or we can trust God to do it. He will let us try as much as we want, but we won't get the results we want until we trust Him to do the work. From my experience, change made because of my nagging or bullying causes resentment and no joy in either of us. Change because of the Holy Spirit's conviction produces lasting, peaceful, and joyful results. Besides, don't we have enough to worry about with just our own behavior? When I am tempted to pay attention to how well I think my husband is doing, I ask myself "How is my love walk?" Our enemy will get us distracted by what our husband is doing or not doing, in order for us to neglect what we are supposed to be doing!

We need to trust in God to meet our needs, not our husband. We don't have to believe that God can't bless us because of him. That's a lie. God will go around our husband to bless us if He needs to.

Stay in peace. Maintaining an atmosphere of peace in our homes is one of the MOST POWERFUL things we can do as a wife and mother. When there is peace in our home, the Holy Spirit has free reign to bless, convict, reprove, enlighten, and guide us and our family into all truth. This does not mean that we "pacify" our husbands or children in order to "keep the peace." That is not real, lasting peace. We must choose to walk in peace by walking in the spirit, staying away from the baits— even in our hearts, and trusting God to lead us in all situations. The peace of God is powerful and when we walk in it, God is free to move on our behalf!

Stay away from the "For Husbands" section. Do not read the For Husbands section and then watch to see if he performs it. That's criticism and judgment! Instead, pray for him, because it will be hard work and praise him when he does something right! Be a cheerleader, not a critic.

Spend a few moments and make some notes on what the Holy Spirit tells you to change in regard to your marriage:

For the Husbands

You are the leader, period. Lead.

Ephesians 5:23 - For the husband is the head of the wife as Christ is the head of the church, his body, of which he is the Savior.

You must give her something to follow.

1 Corinthians 7:33 - But a married man is concerned about the affairs of this world—how he can please his wife

Your prayers are hindered if you are not walking in peace with your wife.

1 Peter 3:7 - Likewise, ye husbands, dwell with them according to knowledge, giving honor unto the wife, as unto the weaker vessel, and as being heirs together of the grace of life; that your prayers be not hindered.

Christ died for the church, so you must put your wife's need before your own.

Ephesians 5:25 - Husbands, love your wives, just as Christ loved the church and gave himself up for her

Live with her according to understanding.

1 Peter 3:7 - Likewise, ye husbands, dwell with them according to knowledge, giving honor unto the wife, as unto the weaker vessel, and as being heirs together of the grace of life; that your prayers be not hindered.

The leader serves all. This establishes follower-ship when each party knows they are being served.

Mark 9:35 - Sitting down, Jesus called the Twelve and said, "If anyone wants to be first, he must be the very last, and the servant of all."

Stay away from the "For Wives" section.

Do not read the For Wives section and then watch to see if she performs it. That's criticism and judgment! Instead, pray for her because it will be hard work and praise her when she does it right! Be a cheerleader, not a critic.

Final Thought The next time your wife or girlfriend gets mad at you over something and you end up being in an argument, what level of leadership will you provide?

Whether she is right or wrong, what does leadership look like at that very moment? Will you let offense make the decision? How about anger? What about bitterness? Will you rise up above your understanding and emotion and lead? What does God say in His word? What are His promises? What does He expect from you? Do you believe He is your reward in the face of injustice? Do you believe His mercies are renewed when YOU choose poorly? What will you believe when your flesh is crying out? What will you do?

Spend a few moments and make some notes on what the Holy Spirit tells you to change in regard to your marriage:

PEACE WITH YOUR CHILDREN

And I will give them one heart and one way, that they may fear Me always, for their own good and for the good of their children after them. Jeremiah 32:38 (NASB)

We must have peace with God and peace with ourselves before we can effectively have peace with our children. If we don't forgive ourselves, and walk in love with ourselves, we can't really do it well with our kids. We can tend to think of our kids as extensions of ourselves. When we aren't walking in love with ourselves, such as overcommitting, not forgiving ourselves, or trying to make others think well of us, we can use our children the same way. We might try using our kids' accomplishments to garner praise for ourselves, or think that their challenges mean we are a failure. These tendencies can make a great relationship with our children hard. Freeing our kids to be who God has created them to be and allowing them to discover who they are in Him is going to be vital for them to grow up feeling loved by God, loved by their parents, and unfettered by our preconceived opinions. They need to find out what they are gifted to do and what they enjoy. We can help by allowing them to try and fail without it becoming a reflection in our minds of our own shortcomings and challenges.

Training Our Children

We are training our children every time we are around them. We are showing them what we value, what we believe is worth spending time on, and what is really important. When we choose to value what God values, we are setting our children up to win in life and be successful (Matthew 6:33). When we choose to attend church regularly, to give tithes and offerings, to walk in love with the unlovely, to freely forgive, we are teaching these values to our children, and they will be blessed! When they see us model unforgiveness and selfishness, those seeds will produce fruit as well. Even when they see us stumbling in an area, such as losing our temper, if they see us repent and forgive one another quickly they learn how to deal with sin correctly. They will understand what mercy and grace are. If we can transfer these eternal truths to our children, they will be so, so blessed!

Our purpose as parents is to

> *Train up a child in the way he should go, even when he is old he will not depart from it. Proverbs 22:6 (NASB)*

and

> *Fathers, do not provoke your children to anger, but bring them up in the discipline and instruction of the Lord. Ephesians 6:4 (NASB)*

There is no more rewarding job in creation than to have and nurture our children. To see them grow more and more into the Godly men and women He created them to be is a delight. As parents, we can very easily carry the weight of responsibility into our hearts over our children, but they are ultimately His and His responsibility. Our job is simply to listen to His leading and obey when it concerns our kids. The results have to be His and His alone. When our kids do well, we praise God for it, knowing that He provided to us anything we were able to contribute. If our kids stumble, we pray and trust, knowing that God cares infinitely more than we do and He has a Master plan! We can't judge the final result of what our kids are becoming before they are "fully cooked." Imagine what one might find in a cocoon of a monarch butterfly before it opens. It would be an ugly, gooey mess! We need to give our kids a break before they are fully transformed as well!

When we are listening to His voice daily in our lives, we are going to hear Him guide us in specific ways that might not seem important at the time, but are building up to something big in the lives of our children. God has given us everything we need in Christ to be an awesome mom or dad for our kids.

Grace and peace be multiplied to you in the knowledge of God and of Jesus our Lord; seeing that His divine power has granted to us everything pertaining to life and godliness, through the true knowledge of Him who called us by His own glory and excellence. For by these He has granted to us His precious and magnificent promises, so that by them you may become partakers of the divine nature, having escaped the corruption that is in the world by lust.
2 Peter 1:2-4 (NASB)

Everything we need "pertaining to life and Godliness" is wrapped up in Him. Becoming a Godly parent definitely fits into this category. He has given us His "precious and magnificent promises" so that we can have a part of His "divine nature." What kind of parent does the Word of God say He is? He is always patient, always kind, and completely forgives His children instantly! Who wouldn't turn out amazingly with this kind of parent? These characteristics are manifested in our lives by the promises of God as we walk in the spirit. What are the promises of God?

Divine Protection of Our Children

See that you do not despise one of these little ones, for I say to you that their angels in heaven continually see the face of My Father who is in heaven. Matthew 18:10 (NASB)

For He will give His angels charge concerning you, to guard you in all your ways. Psalm 91:11 (NASB)

Our children have angels assigned to them. These angels have God's complete attention. They are given the responsibility to guard our children in all their ways. Another thing to consider is this: can we actually control all of the circumstances our children will encounter from their birth until they reach adulthood? Certainly not! It is much better for us, and for them, for us to trust our loving Heavenly Father with the little ones He lends to us. He is really the only one capable of keeping them safe anyway.

We are not advocating a "c'est la vie" attitude that rejects personal responsibility and good parenting over our kids, but when we have done our part, we have to trust God with everything else, and rest. We need to remember that worrying ONLY leads to evil-doing (Psalm 37:8), and we are training our children to trust in God as they see us trust in Him as well.

Spiritual Maturity in Our Children

And all your [spiritual] children shall be disciples [taught by the Lord and obedient to His will], and great shall be the peace and undisturbed composure of your children. Isaiah 54:13 (AMP)

What a great promise! All of our children will be followers of Christ and they will be blessed with "peace and undisturbed composure!" As we train them to follow Jesus, they will learn to trust Him, and that trust produces quiet rest in the midst of life's storms. Jesus promised us that storms (tribulations) would arise from time to time, but what a Godly legacy we can pass on to our children if they can learn from our example to trust God during those times (Psalm 91:2).

Deliverance from Evil

For thus says the Lord: Even the captives of the mighty will be taken away, and the prey of the terrible will be delivered; for I will contend with him who contends with you, and I will give safety to your children and ease them. Isaiah 49:25 (AMP)

Even if our children are currently "captives of the mighty," or "prey of the terrible," they will be delivered! If we will confidently trust and believe that He will contend with those that contend with us, He will give "safety" to our children and "ease them." He can give instant release from negative influences and habits to our children, and complete freedom in Christ to them.

There are many more promises of God in His Word that we can use in our lives to bring freedom and restoration to our children. When we say and believe His Word in our lives, it produces change (Isaiah 55:11).

The Baits and Our Children

James 3:16 tells us,

For wherever there is jealousy (envy) and contention (rivalry and selfish ambition), there will also be confusion (unrest, disharmony, rebellion) and all sorts of evil and vile practices. (AMP)

When we are taking the bait on a continuous basis with our children, and unwilling to apologize and repent, it can lead to the negative things listed. They become confused as they see us walk in unforgiveness, criticism or judgment toward them, but then tell them to walk in forgiveness and mercy. This is the classic "Do as I say, not as I do," scenario, and our children will know it isn't right. If left unchecked and unrepented, these baits then lead to unrest, disharmony, and eventually rebellion as our kids don't trust us anymore to accurately represent the truth to them. We always want our kids to have an open spirit and be willing to receive instruction and correction from us. We need to be sensitive to the Holy Spirit and obey if He encourages us to apologize for our unlovely behavior toward our children or others in their presence. Keeping that openness toward us is a very powerful way to keep an openness in their hearts to other authorities in their lives, especially God. Our children's openness to the moving of the Spirit of God in their lives is worth any amount of "humble pie" we might be asked to eat in order to keep our relationships solid and open.

Let's take a look at how some specific baits work on our flesh and how they can relate to our children.

Worry and Self-Care

When we are worrying about the future of our children and what might happen to them, we have taken the bait. We need to repent of that as soon as we see it, and model for them quiet trust and confidence that God is working all things out for our good and will bless us because He loves us. This will encourage our kids to trust God in their own lives, and they will live successful and blessed.

Jealousy

Our children learn what is important and what is unimportant in life by our examples. When we talk about material possessions, with lust in our hearts, around our children, they learn that "stuff" is what life is all about. When we instead model that our treasure is ultimately in Heaven and that worldly goods and money are just tools we use to love and serve others, they will adopt this value on their own as well.

Unforgiveness

Our children learn how to forgive first by our example of showing forgiveness and mercy to others. When children see a mother and father forgive them and each other freely, they learn to have mercy on others and "give each other a break." Forgiveness is vital to a happy and peaceful home life, because everyone messes up from time to time, and an air of unforgiveness will rob us of sweet peace.

Taking Offense

When our children see us "not easily offended," that will be "normal" for them as well. We must walk in love in front of our children, so they can see what God is like as He loves through us. In our driving, we can just let things go without a word of criticism. As we are shopping at the grocery store, we can patiently wait for our turn at the check out and if the store doesn't have what we need, we can calmly decide to go elsewhere without a work of complaint. This will train our kids to do the same and hold on to the peace Jesus gives us regardless of what circumstances may come!

Criticism, Gossip, Talebearing

When we are critical of others in front of our children, or critical of them, we are operating out of pride instead of love. When our motivation is to bless and edify the hearers like it mentions in Ephesians 4:29, we won't criticize, gossip, or talebear. Many times we are tempted to criticize our children in front of others, but this tears them down and can lead to resentment and bitterness. Instead, let's sow seeds of love and peace, and encourage and bless them with our words.

Judgment

We can't ever really know why our kids do what they do, and to try to do this will not lead us to peace. We need to abandon our pride in this area as well, and walk in love with our children, encouraging them in the Lord to be who they are in Christ. We also need to believe the best about our kids in situations that have previously caused them to stumble. If we automatically assume they are going to fail, we have judged them. Instead, let's allow for the growth we are believing God for and give them a break! If we believe the best, they might just surprise us!

Debate

Children need to know their parents love each other deeply and are committed to each other as well as to them. Watching parents debate various issues over and over can cause them to believe this isn't the case, or that debating is the normal way to communicate with others. We want our kids to feel safe and loved at home. This will keep their spirits open to correction, training, and the Spirit of God moving in their lives.

1. Allow the Holy Spirit to show you where you have "taken the bait" in your relationships with your children and make note of how He wants you to change.

_____

_____

_____

_____

_____

Being a Godly Example

When we see our children struggle in an area we ourselves have struggled in, we can impart to them the wisdom God has given to us in order to overcome it. If we are still working out victory in that area, we can encourage each other in the Lord and pray for one another. We need to remember Hebrews 4:15-16,

> *For we do not have a high priest who cannot sympathize with our weaknesses, but One who has been tempted in all things as we are, yet without sin. Therefore let us draw near with confidence to the throne of grace, so that we may receive mercy and find grace to help in time of need. (NASB)*

Jesus has been through all the temptations and weaknesses we have. He has lived on earth subject to the same flesh that tempts us to become angry, jealous, lustful, and proud, yet He was able to overwhelmingly live in victory in all ways. He didn't do this for Himself. He did this for us! He went through everything we go through on a daily basis, so that He could help us be victorious as well. As parents, by the grace that God provides, we can be the same example and help for our children through any challenge and weakness they encounter. Paul tells the Corinthian church,

> *Be imitators of me, just as I also am of Christ. 1 Corinthians 11:1 (NASB)*

We get to be living examples of Jesus for our children until they are able to successfully follow Him on their own. Even then, if we have developed a strong connection with our children, they will hopefully still be able to look to us for spiritual wisdom and counsel.

Peaceful Adult Relationships

What do we do when we haven't always walked in peace and love with our children and have damaged our relationships to the point where they don't listen to us or respect us?

Let's face it. We all mess up from time to time. Some of us get saved later in life and have a lifetime of decisions we wish we could make again. Let's first establish that there is no condemnation in Christ (Romans 8:1). Every one of us has missed God's perfection by about as far as the earth is from the moon! Let's just start from right here, right now and walk in what God's Word says for us to do. Remember, His Word never returns to Him without accomplishing what He sent it to do (Isaiah 55:11).

> *And we know that God causes all things to work together for good to those who love God, to those who are called according to His purpose. Romans 8:28 (NASB)*

Whatever we have done in our past, if we give it to God and allow Him free reign in our lives, He will turn all these things around for our good and the good of our children. Our children are extremely precious to God. He is a parent too, and knows the grief we feel when our kids stray from His best for them.

We are not left hopeless and helpless in situations involving rebellious children. He has given us His Word to use in faith to accomplish His will! As we are learning to recognize the baits that come to us on a daily basis, we are seeing the schemes of our enemy and are learning to resist him effectively. This same enemy is blinding the eyes of the unrepentant in darkness (2 Corinthians 4:4). As we pray for our children and speak God's Word into their lives, we are shedding light on the darkness. Here are some scriptures that can help us focus our prayers and thinking to agree with God's Word.

But this is what the LORD says: "Yes, captives will be taken from warriors, and plunder retrieved from the fierce; I will contend with those who contend with you, and your children I will save.
Isaiah 49:25 (NIV-1984)

Surely the arm of the LORD is not too short to save, nor his ear too dull to hear. Isaiah 59:1 (NIV-1984)

In the last days, God says, I will pour out my Spirit on all people. Your sons and daughters will prophesy, your young men will see visions, your old men will dream dreams. Acts 2:17 (NIV-1984)

All your sons will be taught by the LORD, and great will be your children's peace. Isaiah 54:13 (NIV-1984)

"As for me, this is my covenant with them," says the LORD. "My Spirit, who is on you, and my words that I have put in your mouth will not depart from your mouth, or from the mouths of your children, or from the mouths of their descendants from this time on and forever," says the LORD. Isaiah 59:21 (NIV-1984)

The entire chapter of Psalm 139 is also a great scripture to meditate on and pray over our children.

How do we walk in peace with our adult children?

When we are no longer in authority over our children, we need to release them to God and trust Him to lead them. If they are still under our roof or relying on us financially, i.e. away at college, we are still in authority and they need to listen and obey our requests. We need to be careful not to try and control their lives, however. Our goal is that when they leave our protection and provision, they are fully equipped to make wise, Godly decisions for themselves. That transition is going to be different for every child as we learn what they are capable of, while allowing them to learn from their mistakes still under our protection and wisdom. It is much better for them to make mistakes and learn while still with us, than for them to learn the "hard way" when there is no safety net of our protection and provision.

How is our relationship with our parents going to look as we try to respect them and still hold our peace?

> *Do not sharply rebuke an older man, but rather appeal to him as a father, to the younger men as brothers, the older women as mothers, and the younger women as sisters, in all purity. 1 Timothy 5:1-2 (NASB)*

Our relationships with our parents are going to look somewhat like our relationships with our adult children in that our goals in both should be respect and edification. We can see in 1 Timothy, that Paul was likening young Timothy's relationship to older men as one of a father-son relationship. Timothy was to "appeal" to the older men and women to obey the Word of God as fathers and mothers. We can infer from this that it is okay for us to "appeal" to our mothers and fathers as well, as long as we are respectful and stay away from debate, criticism, and judgment!

2. Think about your relationships with your parents, in-laws, or older relatives. If any of these relationships need God's peace, write them down here and seek the Lord for how you can start the process of healing them and establishing God's peace.

_____

_____

_____

_____

PRACTICAL PEACE

The things you have learned and received and heard and seen in me, practice these things, and the God of peace will be with you.
Philippians 4:9

While the application of the principles we have shared may be considered personal and individualistic, due to the complexity of your life and personal dynamics, we do have some words of wisdom concerning some common scenarios and questions.

The Media and Peace

When we use the term "Media" we are referring to television and radio, as well as social media websites and services. These services bring their own unique pitfalls when it comes to staying out of strife and staying in peace.

Entertainment

We have many resources for entertainment in our lives, such as movies, internet, television, radio, and more. These tools are wonderful when used by God to transmit the truth of His Word over long distances, but they can become problematic when used as an unfettered conduit for content from the enemy to bring strife right into our midst. We will need to be on guard for what this can mean to our lives. This doesn't mean we aren't allowed to own or use these devices, but rather let's determine not to be on "auto-pilot" and ignore the danger that can come from them. The programming coming through our devices may be littered with things that are contrary to the Word of God, that assail our faith, cast wrong images of marriage (and the Biblical roles designed by God), sex, fidelity, parenting (and the respecting of parents), etc...

Keep and guard your heart with all vigilance and above all that you guard, for out of it flow the springs of life. Proverbs 4:23 (AMPC)

We are free to enjoy various wholesome forms of entertainment—movies, TV, radio, internet—but our attitude always needs to be to guard our hearts first. Even a little bit of filth will leave a mark in our spirit, and it's just not worth the price. This advice is simple—don't trust entertainment and be ready to act, which does include turning it off.

The News

The simple act of watching a news broadcast on TV or listening to talk radio can get us into strife and steal our peace. Why is this so? The very nature of the news is usually to share with us all the things that are going wrong in the world. It is difficult to consume this material without it generating an opinion from us on any one or more of its pieces. This can be a trap for us if we are not careful.

How we handle the news of our current times is between us individually and the Holy Spirit. We may not want to keep watching news on television if we notice our peace level is lower or leaves altogether after we watch it. This may sound odd, but we are prioritizing God's peace and protecting our hearts and our families. It's not worth losing our peace to listen to the latest celebrity gossip or political drama.

The king's heart is like channels of water in the hand of the Lord; He turns it wherever He wishes. Proverbs 21:1 (NASB)

Instead of getting drawn in to having an opinion about what our political leaders say or do, or what is going on in other countries' governments, we can instead appeal to the higher authority that is our Father in heaven. What we think is of no importance, but what He can do as we pray is of eternal importance.

Social Media

Social media has given everyone the ability to communicate with more ease and speed than ever before. It has also made it easier and quicker to get in strife and lose our peace. Social media platforms are amazing communication tools, but we need to know that we are playing with fire and will get burned if we are not careful. The whole experience of these platforms is about our sharing what's going on in our lives and our commenting on what people post about their lives. We need to recognize the potential for strife! Social media makes it easy to chime in on people's lives, and the possibility of offense increases with each interaction.

When there are many words, transgression is unavoidable,
But he who restrains his lips is wise. – Proverbs 10:19 (NASB)

The best advice is to watch out for the baits and to walk in love! Radical, right? We count it as an honor when people "friend us" online because they have given us permission to see into their lives. This is a privilege and a gift from the Lord. He will use us to help those around us, but we cannot help those with whom we are being critical or judgmental.

1. Pay attention this week to how you feel after watching television. Does it bring you peace? Why or why not?

_____

_____

_____

_____

2. How do you feel after having checked Facebook or Twitter?

_____

_____

_____

_____

3. If these things are not bringing you peace, what can you do about it?

_____

_____

_____

Don't Borrow Trouble

We can't adopt the problems of others as our own. Sometimes during our daily activities, we come across the cares and troubles of others. It seems like the "Christian" thing to do in these situations is to take these troubles and burdens on ourselves as well. The Bible tells us to *bear one another's burdens, and thereby fulfill the law of Christ* (Galatians 6:2, NASB)," and to "*weep with those that weep* (Romans 12:15, NASB)." We do not want to get into worry or self-care though, so what is this supposed to look like?

We are told plainly in 1 Peter 5:7 that we are to be,

> *Casting the whole of your care [all your anxieties, all your worries, all your concerns, once and for all] on Him, for He cares for you affectionately and cares about you watchfully. (AMP)*

This doesn't just apply to our own cares, but also the cares of others. Our Father God doesn't want us to carry around the problems of others any more than our own. Once we hear about the troubles and anxieties of another, we should pray and cast that onto our Father God as well. We then have to let it go in our thought life. We need to understand that worrying over others does not equal loving others. If God gives us specific instructions to help in those situations, we must by all means obey, but we are going to be much more able to hear His voice of wisdom when we are not fretting, which ONLY leads to evil (Psalm 37:8)! The enemy may try to use the trials of others to get us to worry, judge, criticize, and condemn. We have to ferociously guard our peace by staying out of worry and strife if we truly want to be used in these situations. If we fall to worry (fret) it leads ONLY to doing evil! Don't do it!

Here is an example of what this might look like. Let's say we hear that our neighbor's father was just put in hospice care, or that our sister just found out she was being laid off of work. If it is appropriate, we could lead these people in prayer over these things, praying the Word of God into their situations. If not, we should pray for them before God in faith using the Word of God. Either way, we are to then "cast our care" and let go of these things in our thought life. Continuing to mull these situations over and trying to figure out how God can solve them, or how we can solve them is worry; and worry is fear, not faith. God has the amazing ability to let us know what we need to do to help, if anything. We need to be completely willing to do whatever He asks of us and then rest, knowing our Father loves us and them and has a wonderful plan for victory for all involved.

The Heat of the Moment

The hardest thing to do is to want to make peace when emotions are hot, and we can barely think or see straight. At this point, we need to get away from that situation, if even for just a few moments. We can excuse ourselves to the restroom or go for a walk, whatever we can do to calm ourselves down. Once we are alone, we can take a few deep breaths and start talking to God. When our mind has been set on the flesh, He can help us turn our minds back to the spirit. He knows what we are going through and really loves us. We need to let the thought of His love for us dwell in our minds. We can remind ourselves that if God is for us who can be against us (Romans 8:31). This is one of the most important things we can do for ourselves because **offenses will come, and how we handle them will directly affect our future**. God has us and our future in the palm of His hand and we need not worry over any part of it. This realization then provides the freedom and security to reach out to someone who has wronged us, knowing that God will make sure our needs are taken care of. This catapults us from the position of a victim into that of a world-changer. The devil hates this because we will be ruining all of his work.

Once we have given our emotions to God and gotten back to peace in the spirit, we can re-engage the other person if necessary. We need to keep ourselves calm and our voice low. It will be very difficult for the other person to escalate the situation if we choose to walk in love and remain calm.

> *A gentle answer turns away wrath, but a harsh word stirs up anger.*
> *Proverbs 15:1 (NIV)*

We need to stay away from the baits like criticism and judgment; instead, we can focus on the facts, and be ready to offer an apology for any misunderstanding. Some conflict is a by-product of poor communication, and if we will take responsibility for our part, it can diffuse a strife-filled situation.

Sometimes things are left unsaid or misinterpreted. This happens all the time. Offering an apology like, "I'm sorry for the miscommunication," can go a long way towards providing peace to a troubled relationship. It's when we decide to be stubborn and unrelenting in our position of "innocence" that things can escalate very quickly.

The Payoff

Sometimes God asks us to walk through difficult situations, and walk in love with challenging people. It might seem easier to just remove ourselves from the situation and go be with other people who like and appreciate us, but submitting to God is the only thing that will produce good results—God's Best for our life. This may sound like a broken record, but this is an important principle. There is nothing more valuable that we could ever obtain in this life than to walk in God's will! Anything else would pale in comparison. Having said that (again), this doesn't necessarily mean we have to be a punching bag for someone else (literally or figuratively). It does mean that we need to be in touch with what God wants us to do. Here's what the Word says:

If it is possible, as far as it depends on you, live at peace with everyone.
Romans 12:18 (NIV)

Just remember, this is for our benefit, not to punish us. There are many situations where we are asked by God to go a little farther than our flesh might like, to absolutely know in our spirits that we have done all we can to make things right. Even when some situations don't end as well as we would like, if we know we have done everything we can to walk in peace, we can walk away satisfied that we did our part. God is faithful to meet our needs, and His peace is what guards our hearts and minds during those times (Phil. 4:7).

Over the course of time, we become accustomed to walking in perpetual peace. As we continue practicing the things the Holy Spirit has taught us in this study, we will start to recognize the spirit of strife when we walk in to a situation. We will start to see it coming, and be able to effectively avoid it as we choose to walk in love and peace instead of taking the baits in the flesh.

4. Are there people in your life that seem to really be able to "push your buttons?"

_____

_____

_____

5. What is it going to cost you to be at peace with these people?

_____

_____

_____

_____

6. Is the peace you will receive worth the sacrifice? Why?

_____

_____

_____

_____

7. What can you do to be better prepared to walk in peace with these people?

_____

_____

_____

_____

THE PURPOSE OF PEACE

So then we pursue the things which make for peace and the building up of one another. Romans 14:19 (NASB)

Peace Prepares Hearts

One purpose for peace in our lives is to allow the good seeds we, and others, have sown into our hearts to germinate, grow, and produce the fruit of righteousness.

And the seed whose fruit is righteousness is sown in peace by those who make peace. James 3:18 (NASB)

When we have heard a great sermon at church, or listened to a great teaching on tape or television, we need to be on our guard against getting into strife. The devil would love to get us upset or angry and steal the word planted in our hearts before it even gets a chance to root and take hold (Mark 4:15). Instead, when we choose to "hold our peace" before and after we hear the Word of God, we are giving the Holy Spirit time to apply His Word to our circumstances and attitudes while adjusting anything He thinks needs attention. The enemy knows this and we see him try especially hard on the way to church, to get everyone upset and "riled up" so that we will be distracted and unable to focus on receiving all God wants for us to have. By purposefully choosing to stay sober and alert, we are choosing peace and preparing the ground in our hearts to accept God's Word for us.

As God is teaching us to remain in His peace in our lives, we need to be sensitive to the areas in which we tend to struggle.

*All discipline for the moment seems not to be joyful, but sorrowful;
yet to those who have been trained by it, afterwards it yields the
peaceful fruit of righteousness. Therefore, strengthen the hands that
are weak and the knees that are feeble, and make straight paths
for your feet, so that the limb which is lame may not be put out
of joint, but rather be healed. Pursue peace with all men, and the
sanctification without which no one will see the Lord.
Hebrews 12:11-14 (NASB)*

The writer of Hebrews encourages us to "make straight paths for your feet, so that the limb which is lame may not be put out of joint." He is saying that we need to keep ourselves away from temptation as much as possible, until we learn how to effectively resist it. An example of this would be for an alcoholic to stay out of situations in which he would have traditionally taken a drink of alcohol, such as in a bar or club. As he is learning new behaviors, it is vital to his success to stay away from old drinking buddies and the environments that foster his addiction. We can apply this same principle to our walk in peace.

As we are learning new behaviors such as not gossiping or judging, it may be necessary for us to avoid the people in our lives that encouraged us to "take the bait." We may need to "make straight paths for our feet" by walking away from strife-filled conversations or not taking phone calls from people that like to debate with us over politics or religion. We find that after we have learned to effectively hold our peace on a regular basis, God tends to bring us back to the very people that were negatively influencing us in order for us to influence them in a positive way as we walk in the spirit and powerful peace!

Once we can bring His presence to others with whom we come in contact, He can move in their lives to bring them to peace with God as well.

1. Are there any areas in your life in which you are struggling to see victory in your walk toward powerful peace?

_____

_____

_____

_____

2. How can you make straight paths for yourself in these areas?

_____

_____

_____

_____

_____

Peace Makes Us Vessels of Honor

All of us want God to use us in powerful ways to help others in our lives, but many of us don't realize that how we are used by God has more to do with our behavior than anything else.

> *Now in a large house there are not only gold and silver vessels, but also vessels of wood and of earthenware, and some to honor and some to dishonor. Therefore, if anyone cleanses himself from these things, he will be a vessel for honor, sanctified, useful to the Master, prepared for every good work. 2 Timothy 2:20-21 (NASB)*

What are the "things" Paul is referring to here that we are to cleanse ourselves of? He tells us a few verses before this.

> *Remind them of these things, and solemnly charge them in the presence of God not to wrangle about words, which is useless and leads to the ruin of the hearers. Be diligent to present yourself approved to God as a workman who does not need to be ashamed, accurately handling the word of truth. But avoid worldly and empty chatter, for it will lead to further ungodliness, and their talk will spread like gangrene. 2 Timothy 2:14-17 (NASB)*

Paul is charging Timothy and others in his church to stay away from strife-filled speech! Walking in the spirit and staying out of debate, gossip, and talebearing is crucial for us to be used as "vessels of honor."

What does Paul mean when he says "some to honor and some to dishonor" concerning the vessels in a house? In ancient times, there were many uses for vessels in a home. The vessels used in the preparation of food or for entertainment would be considered "vessels for honor," and could be overlaid with gold or silver. The vessels used for trash or the toilet were of a poorer quality and were considered to be used "to dishonor." This is where the analogy of gossip as vomit is helpful! The Lord is telling us here that if we want Him to be able to use us as a blessing in the lives of those around us, and not just be a toilet bowl, we have to cleanse ourselves of our worldly habits and attitudes and put on the peace of God. God isn't going to use trash cans to serve His good Word to others. Paul continues in verses 22 and 23 by saying,

> *Now flee from youthful lusts and pursue righteousness, faith, love, and peace, with those who call on the Lord from a pure heart. But refuse foolish and ignorant speculations, knowing that they produce quarrels. (NASB)*

God takes debate and other strife-filled speech very seriously and **will not use us** for honorable ministry to others if we continue in these behaviors.

3. Who determines whether we are used by God in powerful ways in the lives of others?

_____

_____

_____

_____

_____

Many times we believe that our past failures make us unqualified to be used by God in any meaningful ways. We are tempted to think that because we have been divorced, had an abortion, taken drugs, been to prison, been abused, or any number of other reasons, we are disqualified from powerful ministry in the body of Christ. We serve such an amazing God! He doesn't look at our abilities, our past, or our sins when determining His plans for us.

Let's look at King David from the Old Testament. He committed adultery with Bathsheba, made her pregnant, then had her husband killed to cover it up! David was far from perfect, but let's read in Acts what the Holy Spirit has to say about him.

For David, after he had served God's will and purpose and counsel in his own generation, fell asleep [in death] and was buried among his forefathers. Acts 13:36 (AMP)

Even though David murdered and committed adultery, the Holy Spirit says he "served God's will and purpose and counsel in his own generation!" I think we would all be happy with that epitaph!

So, why didn't David's past prevent him from being used by God? How was David able to do this in light of his sins? To find out, let's look at one of the Psalms he wrote.

Bless the Lord, O my soul,

And all that is within me, bless His holy name.

Bless the Lord, O my soul,

And forget none of His benefits;

Who pardons all your iniquities,

Who heals all your diseases;

Who redeems your life from the pit,

Who crowns you with lovingkindness and compassion;

Who satisfies your years with good things,

So that your youth is renewed like the eagle.

Psalm 103:1-5 (NASB)

David didn't look to himself for vindication and righteousness... he looked to God. He knew that the good things he received from God were not based on his own behavior, but on God's goodness and mercy.

Someone else who was used mightily by God in spite of his own murders and enmity toward Christ was the Apostle Paul, who even says of himself,

This is a faithful saying and worthy of all acceptance, that Christ Jesus came into the world to save sinners, of whom I am chief. - 1 Timothy 1:15 (NKJV)

So how were David and Paul able to do all they did in spite of some very serious transgressions? They relied not on their own abilities and gifts, but on the grace of God in them.

For I am the least of the apostles, who am not worthy to be called an apostle, because I persecuted the church of God. But by the grace of God I am what I am, and His grace toward me was not in vain; but I labored more abundantly than they all, yet not I, but the grace of God which was with me. 1 Corinthians 15:9-10 (NKJV)

David and Paul didn't look to themselves for the ability to lead God's people. They looked to God to provide the grace to cause His will to be done in their lives. God included their testimonies in the Bible on purpose, because He wants to do the same thing through us. As we abide in Jesus, we will follow in their footsteps and be able to fulfill God's will, purpose, and counsel in our lives as well.

And God is able to make all grace abound toward you, that you, always having all sufficiency in all things, may have an abundance for every good work. 2 Corinthians 9:8 (NKJV)

I told you at the beginning of this book about my decision as a young 18 yea-old to completely follow the will of God for my life. I mentioned that after 15 years or so of trying to control my family, my friends, my flesh, and my circumstances, I finally gave up! I was exhausted and unsuccessful. I finally learned that it was never about my own ability anyway. It was my foolish pride that thought I could do anything with my life based on my own strength of will or resolve. I finally came to the place of trusting, not only what He had done on the cross, but His daily guidance and grace to fulfill His purposes in my life. The truth is, we are ALL exceedingly messed up, so He gets the glory and praise when we trust Him and He leads us into triumph and victory! —Sharon

We can't let the enemy tell us that our past or our weaknesses disqualify us any longer. Every one of us has something in our past that would disqualify us before God, if He was going to look at our behavior to determine our worth as a "vessel of honor." The blood of Jesus has made us righteous before God's eyes. It is a good thing to remember, though, that we can cause ourselves to be a "vessel for dishonor" if we walk in the flesh and reject peace with others in our speech. We need to walk in the spirit so we stay out of strife, and He will be able to use us as mighty vessels of peace!

4. What in your past have you been allowing to disqualify you for God's perfect will, purpose, and counsel in your life?

_____

_____

_____

_____

_____

5. What are you going to believe now?

_____

_____

_____

_____

_____

You have now read all of Powerful Peace and have some revelation on how to walk in peace consistently in your life. I believe you are starting to see more and more of God's blessings on you and your family as a result. The temptation will be to share this message with everyone willing to listen, but I would like to offer a word of wisdom to you in the form of a true story.

One afternoon as I was working in my yard, I noticed some bare spots in the grass and went to the local garden store to pick up some grass seed. I found the right kind and a good reputable brand and purchased a small bag that was more than enough for my needs. After I got home and spread it in the bare spots in my yard, I noticed some bare spots in my neighbors yard and thought it would be a nice Christian thing to do to apply some grass seed to their yard as well. Over the next week or so, I faithfully watered my seeds and the seeds in my neighbors yard daily. I started to see some green and felt pride in knowing I had not only looked well after my yard, but I had blessed my neighbor as well. After a few more days, however, I looked closely at the sprouts coming up and they weren't baby grass sprouts at all!!! I waited a few more days and some weird weeds were growing! The seeds I had planted had looked exactly like grass seeds! The bag clearly stated they were brand name grass seeds! I ran to my neighbors yard and I was horrified! I had unknowingly sown weeds into their yard!

I was able to easily kill the weeds with weed-killer, and planted a new batch of true grass seeds. As I was meditating on this and asked the Lord about it, He told me the lesson I needed to learn. In our spiritual life and growth, we will come across many teachings and messages. They may look like and be labelled as "Christian" or "Inspirational," but it is vitally important for us to test the seeds that others would introduce into our hearts before we plant an entire crop in our hearts, and especially in the hearts and minds of our neighbors, friends, and family members. Once we have tried the precepts and lessons we have learned in our own hearts and minds, and have proven the truth with the Word of God and the usefulness of the message with experience, we will be able to effectively share the message with others with wisdom and authority. Test the seeds in your own life before you sow them!
—Sharon

Footnotes

1. strife. (n.d.). Collins English Dictionary - Complete & Unabridged 10th Edition. Retrieved September 19, 2012, from Dictionary.com website: http://dictionary.reference.com/browse/strife

2. envy. (n.d.). Collins English Dictionary - Complete & Unabridged 10th Edition. Retrieved September 19, 2012, from Dictionary.com website: http://dictionary.reference.com/browse/envy

3. worry. (n.d.). Dictionary.com Unabridged. Retrieved September 19, 2012, from Dictionary.com website: http://dictionary.reference.com/browse/worry

4. condemn. (n.d.). Dictionary.com Unabridged. Retrieved September 19, 2012, from Dictionary.com website: http://dictionary.reference.com/browse/condemn

5. gossip. (n.d.). Dictionary.com Unabridged. Retrieved September 19, 2012, from Dictionary.com website: http://dictionary.reference.com/browse/gossip